LOCKED IN

ONE MAN'S MIRACULOUS ESCAPE FROM THE TERRIFYING CONFINES OF

LOCKED IN

SYNDROME

Richard Marsh
with Jeff Hudson

piatkus

PIATKUS

First published in Great Britain in 2014 by Piatkus

Copyright © Richard Marsh and Jeff Hudson 2014

The moral right of the authors has been asserted.

A CIP catalogue record for this book
is available from the British Library.

ISBN 978-0-349-40143-0

Typeset in Swift by M Rules
Printed and bound in Great Britain by
Clays Ltd, St Ives plc

Papers used by Piatkus are from well-managed forests
and other responsible sources.

MIX
Paper from
responsible sources
FSC www.fsc.org   FSC® C104740

Piatkus
An imprint of
Little, Brown Book Group
100 Victoria Embankment
London EC4Y 0DY

An Hachette UK Company
www.hachette.co.uk

This book is dedicated to Lili, my girls
and all my friends who played such an
important role in my recovery.

Contents

Acknowledgements

Of course I must thank my wife Lili and my daughters Michelle, Shannon and Melanie. I absolutely could not have made it through such a difficult time without their love and support. David and Colleen Topper, Keith and Pam Reuter – what beautiful friends: the Toppers and Reuters consistently made the one-hour drive to visit me while I was in Care Meridian. My friend of 55 years, Steve Logan, travelled 750 miles to visit me in the ICU when he heard I had a stroke. I must acknowledge Lili's friends Pat Sweigert and Angela Fontana, who provided so much help, support and love to her after her world was turned upside down. I can't say thank you enough to my physical therapist, Dennis, and my occupational therapist, Christie, at Care Meridian. They believed in my ability to recover and made me believe in it too. And thank you to my angels at Care Meridian, Margarita and Arthur: they were my primary nurse's aids, caring for my everyday needs with great care and humour. I must thank Melanie Romain, my speech therapist, who taught me to speak again. I also want to thank her for the cheeseburger she smuggled in to me when I was able to start eating solid foods again.

There are four people who were instrumental in making this book a reality and who deserve a big thank-you. Margo Sinclair

Savell believed in the need to tell my story and was responsible for opening the door that made it possible. Amelia Hill from the *Guardian* newspaper in London reported my story and, as a result, I met my literary agent, David Riding of MBA Literary Agents, Ltd. David also saw the need for my story to be told and put in motion the process of creating this book. Since I'm not a writer, David introduced me to Jeff Hudson. Jeff listened to my story, then did an amazing, wonderful job in writing this book. He was able to capture my feelings and emotions as if he was by my side through the entire experience. Thank you, Jeff. You are awesome.

Don't Do It

'Don't do it! I'm begging you, don't. Please don't kill me!'

There are no two ways around it. The man in the white coat wants to end my life. He's made it perfectly clear. He knows what to do and he's prepared to go ahead without a second thought. It doesn't seem to matter to him that I'm screaming as loud as I can, imploring him to let me live. Nothing matters to him. The man is acting as though I'm not even here.

And the worst thing is, the only person in the world who could stop him vowed to me years ago that she would never try . . .

CHAPTER ONE

I Think I'm Having a Stroke

It's so dark. Dark and quiet. It must be the middle of the night.

Then why is it so damn hot in here?

Is there anything worse than burning up in bed? I hate that. I've always hated it. Ever since I was a little kid. I guess that's the downside of growing up in a desert ...

It was a Wednesday. I didn't expect to die that day. No one expects to die on a Wednesday.

And definitely not while doing that job.

I was a sixty-year-old high school teacher and I'd never felt better. Working part time gave me the freedom to ride my Harley, read, play guitar and tend my vegetable garden – all great solitary pastimes. My health meant everything to me. I cooked my own produce, I avoided saturated fat and fast food of any kind, and I worked out every day in the gym, as I had for more than forty years. I'd even met my wife, Lili, working out. I'd been called restless but never reckless. I didn't ride the Harley anywhere near its 1360cc capacity, despite the voice of my old childhood friend Robert 'Evel' Knievel ringing in my ears, urging me to open up the throttle on every trip. I had a nice life, a comfortable life, a *safe* life. After the job I used to have, teaching was a blessing.

For twenty-five years it had all been so different. Serving as a police officer in Napa Valley, California, and Cape Cod, Massachusetts, and then Sheriff of Clay County, Nebraska, my life had felt anything but safe. From the high-speed chases and the stand-offs with armed felons to driving into the heart of gang territory to make an arrest on my own, I, like all of my colleagues, put my life on the line for the greater good every time I pulled on the uniform. In the heat of the moment I never thought of the danger. Maybe I even enjoyed it a little. Nothing beats that adrenaline rush of being fired at by a suspect unknown while you're screaming into your radio for the back-up that just won't come.

But police work is a young man's game. I always knew that. If you're still alive after twenty years it's time to get out, and that's what I had done. I was fifty-five and I'd made it; I'd served my time and I'd emerged unscathed. I'd even, I hoped, done some good along the way. I was ready for a new, quieter, safer life. What I didn't know was that after years of facing death for a living, the biggest threat to my life would come from my own body.

What time is it? This heat is killing me.

I can't see the clock on my bedside table. Maybe there's been a power cut. That would explain the blackness outside. Even through drapes I can normally make out the streetlamps.

I try to swing out of bed and realise I can't move. That's interesting. Am I not really awake? That would explain everything. The darkness, the heat, the quiet – they're all in my imagination. It's just a dream. When I wake up all will be right with the world . . .

Leaving the police service, like leaving the armed forces, poses certain problems. I still wanted to work but I feared that nothing out there in the civilian world was going to fill the void created when I handed in my badge. It was by sheer coincidence that the man who'd originally found me a post at Napa PD, Randy Fitt, got in touch again.

'There's a vacancy at Napa High School for a forensic science teacher,' he said, ever the fount of police knowledge.

'Why are you telling me?'

'I think you should apply. Put that brain of yours to some use.'

'I don't know, Randy. I hear the money's not too good in teaching.'

'So do it for the good of your soul!'

I was right about the money, but I got paid in ways I could never have imagined. I'd started and ended my police career in Napa, but during my years away the city had become overrun by gangs, particularly the Norteños – whose members were identifiable by the red they wore – from the north of the region, and the blue-adorned Sureños from the south. Muggings, thefts, murders – you name it, they were responsible. Every time I flipped the handcuffs onto a perpetrator, a little more of the dwindling sympathy I felt for them evaporated.

Then I walked into Napa High School on my first day and I was the one who learned a valuable lesson as my past and future collided.

I was given directions to a classroom down the hall, so I made my way to where thirty sixteen-year-olds were waiting. There was no getting away from it: I was scared as hell. An armed gang I could handle. But kids? What was I letting myself in for? I reached the room, took a deep breath and pulled open the door.

Then I froze.

All my training came flooding back. In the next instant I imagined myself retreating behind the door, pulling out my gun, clicking my radio and calling for back-up.

'This is an emergency. Gangbangers. Assistance required now!'

Then I looked again. Yes, the entire back row of the classroom comprised young kids wearing red bandannas. And, yes, the front row was a sea of blue. And, yes, they were all members of the gangs who'd given me so much trouble over the years. But right there, right then, they were just young kids at school.

And they'd come to take my class.

For perhaps the first time in my life I saw the problem law enforcement had with the Sureños and Norteños. They were all just kids, or at least they were when they joined the gangs. They sat together in class, they had their own little cliques in the canteen and they hung around together after school. But they were just kids looking for direction. If the police couldn't give them that, then maybe the education system could.

I knew then I'd made the right decision, and not only for the good of my soul.

I'm serving the community again. I am going to make a difference.

This is not a dream. So what is it, then? Everything is a jumble. I guess I'm not well. That would explain why I can't see. Have I been injured?

I'm a police officer, after all. Danger is part of the job description. So, have I been shot?

But wait. That's not right. I quit the department years ago. Or did I? Did I really leave or was I killed in action?

Am I alive or dead?

It had all begun the day before, on Tuesday, 19 May 2009. Lili and I were following our usual routine. Among all the other things I loved about her, she had dedicated her life to serving the community. When we'd met four years earlier she had been working as a midwife, delivering babies into the world in a private practice. Now she was working at the other end of the age spectrum as a nurse at Napa Valley Hospice. In between she'd worked at our local medical centre, Queen of the Valley. She'd helped so many people at the start of life and at the end. I liked that about her. She liked the fact that I helped the ages in between. The two of us had pretty much the whole age spectrum covered.

Tuesday was a teaching day. Same as Monday, Wednesday, Thursday and Friday. As I woke up, I heard Lili returning from her early-morning gym session. That was normal. I made myself breakfast, showered, dressed and pottered about the house till it was time for us both to leave for work. The hospice was about two miles away. School was approximately the same distance in the other direction. Lili took the car, a lovely red Mustang; I rode my motorbike as usual. Two miles is barely enough distance to warm up the engine, but I liked rolling into school on two wheels. I'd had bikes all my life but there was certainly something cool about pulling up on a Harley. Some kids stared openly. Others looked only when they thought I couldn't see. But everyone heard me coming, I knew that. Everyone hears a Harley.

I checked my messages in the staff room, had a coffee with a few of the other teachers and went over my notes for the morning's lesson. More of the normal routine.

Then I went down the corridor, yanked open the door and started pulling out my latest blood-splatter slides, videotapes and phials of a thick, dark red unguent. Today was going to be a practical lesson. We'd be recreating blood patterns from actual crime scenes and looking for clues that would help secure a prosecution. Was the blood dropping straight down? Was the person moving at a high or low velocity? What kind of blood are we looking at? What pattern is the blood forming? Was anything or anyone else involved? It was real *CSI* stuff and I knew that if the class enjoyed it half as much as I always did, we were in for a good lesson.

They loved it. There was fake blood everywhere. On desks, in books and all over their clothes, but no one minded. Not even the Sureños – and if there's one group who do not like wearing red, it's them.

Blood patterns can tell you so much – angle of shot, velocity of victim in relation to the perpetrator, who was standing where, what shape the victim was in when he was shot. Thanks to the colour and texture of the blood you can even make a pretty informed guess at what time it all happened. Sniper shot or point-blank hit, victim backing away or on the attack, self-defence or intent.

'You just have to work through the clues,' I said. 'The answers are all there if you know where to look.'

And I *did* know where to look. In fact, I knew everything there was to know about blood. I was pretty sure of that. I'd seen it on ceilings, I'd seen it on railway tracks, I'd seen whole apartments decorated in the stuff. I'd seen men look almost hollow they'd lost so much. I'd seen hearts on pavements, brains on windows. I'd seen blood on walls, on doors, on people, on pets. There wasn't anything I hadn't seen.

Or so I thought.

There was just one scenario I didn't share with the class. One crime scene I omitted. The one where the blood didn't splatter. The one where it stayed inside the victim's body and attacked without mercy or motive.

In less than twenty-four hours, I would learn more than I ever wished to know about that particular scenario.

I'm pretty sure I just saw a flicker of light. A definite spark. Something in front of me is coming into focus. Are my eyes just acclimatising to the dark or is it actually getting lighter?

I can hear something, too. Voices, people.

I can almost make out a shape in front of me. Is it my wife? Is that why she's not lying next to me?

I see her. It's definitely Lili. But who is she with? And why are they in our bedroom?

Too late. It's dark again and I . . .

Want . . .

To . . .

Sleep . . .

I was unusually ratty that Tuesday. I remember being short with the class and annoyed with myself even as I was doing it. You introduce practical aspects, especially messy ones, into a group of teenagers and you're going to get a certain amount of fallout. Noise levels, excitement, behaviour – they all take a turn for the worse. Usually I was on top of that, steering the exuberance into a direction I could manage. That Tuesday I tried to clamp down on anyone who spoke out of turn. And for some reason it really got to me when they started packing their books away before the midday bell. I felt myself beginning to boil.

Why would I do that? It wasn't me. I didn't like it. It wasn't how I taught.

It wasn't *normal*.

Brrrriiiiiing.

Saved by the bell. Literally. The kids went off to eat in their blue and red halves of the canteen – although how they had an appetite after what I'd just shown them defeated me – and I got ready to leave, everything forgotten. I had only the one class on a Tuesday. The afternoon was my own. A few errands, then home. What could be better? As I rode my bike out onto Jefferson Street, the Californian sun beating down on my back, I didn't have a care in the world.

A few years earlier I might have grumbled my way around the local stores as I did the shopping. But with Lili working longer hours than me, and with teaching so much less stressful than police work, it was the natural thing to do in my free time. And in any case, every errand I ran gave me another chance to fire up the Harley.

Tempting as it was to take off for the highways and mountains to enjoy some speed and make Evel proud, I got just as much satisfaction heading home. East Avenue runs north to south through Napa. It's the main street through the Alta Heights area and it can be busy. But as I sat indicating to turn into our driveway, I didn't care about the traffic or the fact that our neighbours' houses were too close for my liking. All I could see was the beautiful old oak tree, at least the same age as our seventy-year-old house, and behind it the lavender and rose bushes in full bloom. I smiled.

Nature is a wonderful thing.

As much as I loved being on the bike, I was already picturing myself tending the vegetable garden around the back for the next couple of hours.

I'd never realised how much I enjoyed my own company until Lili pointed it out to me soon after we met. She said she'd never known anyone as comfortable in their own body as me. Even at work it was just me in a patrol car or me in a classroom.

'You really don't need anyone at all, do you?' Lili teased.

'I need you.'

'Ha, we'll see.'

I thought of that from time to time, usually after realising I'd just spent two or three hours without seeing another human being and it hadn't bothered me one bit. I think it's good for your soul to be by yourself for a while, to have your own thoughts. Still, even a solitary man needs a companion.

When Lili came home, she showered and joined me for the dinner I'd already prepared.

'What would I do without you?' she said, kissing me as she took her place at the table.

The previous owner had remodelled the house from a series of small rooms to create a more open feel. From my seat I could see the kitchen and the lounge area. It made a small area feel spacious and welcoming.

Afterwards Lili turned on the TV and I grabbed a book – another solitary pastime I couldn't live without – and another perfect evening passed. By eight o'clock Lili was ready to hit the sack. Getting up at four to go to the gym before work took its toll. I lasted another couple of hours – about a dozen chapters – before turning in.

A few niggles with my students aside, it had been a typical Tuesday. Not much happening, but all I needed to be perfectly content. That was my life at sixty.

There's a light at the end of the tunnel. The flickering is back. I can see it in the distance, on and off, guiding me. I want to see more.

I wish I knew what was going on. Is my wife still here? Is she protecting me? Am I safe?

Or is that light at the end of the tunnel on the front of a train which is about to flatten me?

Sometimes I hear Lili's alarm go, sometimes I don't. At 4 a.m. on Wednesday, 20 May 2009, I was dead to the world.

The first thing I noticed as I stirred was the smell of coffee wafting across the open-plan living area. I smiled.

Lili must be back from the gym.

The clatter of bowls and cutlery from the kitchen confirmed it. Prising my eyes open, I checked the clock. It was 6.45. Time I was making a move as well.

While showering is one of the great modern pleasures, shaving is always a chore. Every day for forty-five years and it's never got any more enjoyable. But this time, as I stared through the steam into the bathroom mirror, it was even worse than usual. Something wasn't right.

I wasn't right.

I searched my mind for what the problem might be. *I must have had the shower too hot again.* That was nothing new. The scorching water often triggered a short bout of light-headedness.

But as I doused my baby-smooth face with cold water I realised there was nothing familiar about the sensation I was feeling today. I wasn't light-headed. I wasn't nauseous. I felt no pain. But something was wrong. I just couldn't put my finger on what it was.

I continued my morning routine as best I could. Lili knocked on the door and asked if I wanted coffee.

'I'm fine, thanks,' I replied, even though I was anything but.

'Are you all right, honey?' she asked, looking me up and down as I joined her in the kitchen.

'I'm feeling ...' I paused, searching for the right word. 'I'm feeling *weird*.'

'Why don't you sit down?'

Sit down? Yes, why don't I do that?

I slumped onto the couch in our front room. Had I picked up

a bug? Working in a school, you are subjected to lots of viruses. I let my thoughts and hands drift to my thighs, my stomach, my chest, like a full-body scan. I wasn't sick. I didn't have a stomach upset. It wasn't a migraine. So what was it?

'Rich?'

I looked up and realised Lili had been standing in front of me for a while.

'Sorry?'

'I said, do you want me to stay home with you today?'

I swatted the idea away. 'No, no, it'll pass. Whatever this is, it won't keep me down for long.'

'Okay, well, if you're sure.'

When she leaned down to kiss me goodbye, I still felt in control. I could see the picture window opposite and hear the traffic filtering past the house as people made their way to school and work.

Then Lili closed the front door behind her and my whole world fell in.

I don't know what caused the change, but the second that door shut, I could no longer make out the photographs of Hawaii on the wall or lift my legs onto the small footstool next to the sofa. Every thought I had was about what was wrong with me, every part of my body focused on how I might get better. I didn't hear Lili's car pull out of the driveway. I didn't hear the coffee percolator, even though I knew it must still be bubbling. I couldn't even make out my own feet in front of me.

This is more than feeling weird.

I was still none the wiser, but I had a very bad feeling about what was happening. Some silent assassin was in the room with me. The blows could come from anywhere. I was on guard, alert, but frozen at the same time.

My police medical training was first-aid-based. Whatever was happening to me was well beyond that sphere of learning. Maybe Lili was still in the driveway?

I managed to get to my feet and felt the earth spin. A head-rush can happen to anyone who stands too suddenly, but this was much worse. I flicked my hand out to the wall. Instinctively, I knew I couldn't balance. My legs felt like they would give way any second.

This is serious. I need a doctor.

No, I needed a nurse. One in particular.

I need Lili.

I could see the telephone on the desk in the dining area, about fifteen feet away from where I was standing. On a normal day I could be there in under five seconds. If I vaulted the table I could reach it in two.

Vault the table? What the hell was my brain thinking? My body was in no condition to vault anywhere. I was struggling just to stay upright. If I stopped leaning against the wall, I would surely hit the floor.

But I had to reach that phone.

I focused on my right leg and told it to move. I felt it swing forward about six inches, but it was lumpen, heavy. Like it didn't belong to me at all. When I tried to move my left leg, it wouldn't budge. My weight was spread across my right leg and my hand on the wall. I knew then the only way I was going to be able to move was if I let go of the wall.

But that's the only thing keeping me up.

Now I was scared. But what terrified me even more was Lili coming home that night and finding me unconscious on the floor. Whatever was happening to me, I was pretty sure that was how it would end – if I didn't get to that phone.

'Come on, Rich,' I shouted at myself. 'You can do this!'

Three, two, one ...

I pushed my hand against the wall and used the momentum to swing my left leg forward ... then my right, then my left, then my right. I was moving. It wasn't pretty, but I was moving.

Too fast.

I'd gone only a few steps but the top of my body was beginning to overtake the bottom. This could end only one way unless I took control. I started to windmill my arms for balance like a little kid running down a hill, but it wasn't enough. I managed to force another long stride out of my legs, but then collapsed against the back of a chair. I gripped it so hard that both hands hurt, but at least it propped me up. That was my main priority now.

I have to stay on my feet.

I knew if I hit the floor it would be game over.

I'd covered six feet but it felt like six miles. And I still had nine feet to go. But at least I now had the furniture to help.

Pushing myself off the chair, I let my momentum propel me towards the table. Hands gripping the edge for dear life, I inched around one whole side. It seemed to take for ever, but I managed it. The phone was almost in reach, teasing me from the desk, daring me to pick it up.

I took a deep breath. The desk was only four feet away but there was nothing between me and it. No chairs, no walls, no tables. I was going to have to do this on my own.

For a split second, it felt like my balance had returned. I moved one leg and it went exactly where I'd told it to go. Was my problem disappearing? I didn't have time to dwell on it.

It was now or never!

In my mind, I covered the final few feet like Usain Bolt. In reality, I must have looked like Frankenstein's monster on ice. But I made it. I retained control over my legs just long enough to reach the desk and collapse into the chair.

It was a huge relief to learn that whatever was wrong with me did not seem to be affecting my fine motor skills. I flicked through the phone's directory and quickly found Lili's work number. I pressed the dial button and waited impatiently for someone to pick up.

A familiar voice on the hospice switchboard answered.

'It's Rich,' I said. 'Has Lili arrived yet?'

'I'm sorry? Who is this?'

I repeated myself. But the woman on the other end of the line didn't seem to understand a word I was saying.

What's wrong with you? Don't you speak English? What's not to understand?

I was losing patience and knew I was running out of time. The phone grew heavy in my hand.

'Look, please just tell Lili to call me. It's simple. Please just tell her, okay?' I hung up, desperate.

Less than a minute later the phone rang.

'Rich?'

It was Lili.

'Rich, are you all right?'

'Come home,' I said. 'Please come home.'

'Rich?'

Not you as well. What's wrong with this damn phone?

Before I could try again she said, 'Stay where you are. I'm coming home.'

I couldn't help smiling, even as I heard the call disconnect. My Lili was coming home. At that moment, getting hold of my wife, seeing her face, feeling her arms around me seemed the most important thing in the world. It had never even crossed my mind to call 911.

Looking back, I still don't understand why I didn't try to make that second call. I had seen enough tragedy in my professional life to recognise a life-threatening incident. I clearly wasn't thinking straight. Not only could I have called an ambulance myself, I could have stayed right where I was. The desk chair was comfortable and it was keeping me upright. I was conscious. I should have just sat tight and waited.

But I didn't do that.

The dining room was at the front of the house. The front door was only ten feet away. I'd already covered more than that to reach the phone. I could get there, couldn't I?

I still don't know why I bothered. Of course, Lili had her own key. And even if she forgot it, the mood she was in, she would have kicked down the door without a second thought. But at the time it seemed important for me to reach that door.

It was easier to get up this time. My balance was still okay. The lead weights at the ends of my legs were more manageable. I started to think that maybe the dizziness was just a passing phase. But just as I pulled open the door, everything disappeared again. My balance, my coordination, my strength. It was like they were all instantly switched off.

At least I still had my hearing. The sound of distant sirens filled the air. After years in the force, I could identify exactly which emergency vehicles were approaching. I could picture the red and blue lights flashing, bright even in daytime. I knew they were heading my way.

Seconds later there was a squeal of rubber as the first emergency vehicle pulled to a halt just beyond the oak at the top of our drive. It wasn't an ambulance but a fire truck. Ambulances in

America are usually manned by EMTs – emergency medical technicians – whereas firefighters are highly trained paramedics so they are often also alerted when lives are in danger, fire or no fire. In a nutshell, in most states, firefighters are authorised to 'break the skin' when giving treatment, whether with a needle or an intravenous lifeline, while EMTs are not.

At that moment, I really didn't care which of the emergency services had arrived first. It was the third vehicle screeching to a stop further down the road that held my attention. I didn't even look in the paramedics' direction as they leapt out of their cab, medical bags in hand. Nor was I interested in the gurney being dragged out of the back of the ambulance by the EMTs. I only had eyes for the woman sprinting down the driveway.

I'd asked Lili to come home and she had. I knew she would reach me before any of the first responders, even though she'd been the last to arrive.

'Rich!' she called out. 'Are you okay? What's going on?'

I hated seeing her so anxious but I couldn't hide what was happening any longer. Not from her, and not from myself.

'Lili,' I slurred. 'I think I'm having a stroke.'

CHAPTER TWO

Has He Been Drinking?

The first thing I see is a TV.

It's not my TV. This isn't my room, not even my house.

Where am I?

It's a hospital room.

I remember now. I remember everything.

The time bomb was ticking from the moment I was born.

The thing that would one day cause experienced doctors to pronounce me 'clinically dead' had been with me from the very beginning. My own doctor was unaware of it. And so, of course, were my parents, my teachers and me. I managed to live a full and happy life, with four wives and three wonderful, beautiful daughters, before I had the first sign. But when it came, it came quickly and brutally.

I never should have stood a chance.

I know that voice.

Lili.

Thank God. Even though I can't see her, if she's talking to me, I must be all right.

Wait. She's not talking to me. My vision's coming back. Someone else is in the room, just outside my peripheral vision. Lili's talking to her.

About me.

'I should have stayed at home. I knew he wasn't right.'

'It's not your fault. You couldn't have known.'

The other voice is familiar. I can't put a name to it, though. Or a face. My head is so fuzzy. I guess it must be a doctor. Or a nurse.

'How did you find out?'

'He called me at work. It's only a five-minute drive but I was still in the car park when he rang.'

'Why didn't he call 911 himself?'

'He used to be 911. Maybe he's never called them before.'

No, that wasn't the reason. I wanted to hear Lili's voice. She'd know what to do. I was sure of that. Everything would be all right if I just heard her voice.

I just wanted her to come home.

'We need to get him sitting down.'

Strong hands gripped under my arms and I was carried upright back into the house, my feet touching the floor but contributing little to my movement. Lili scampered ahead to give directions, then stood aside.

'Hey, guys, I recognise him,' one of the EMTs said. 'This is Richard Marsh, retired Police Department.'

He instinctively looked to Lili for confirmation. She nodded. I recognised the EMT from a grisly case a few years back, but the firefighters and the other EMT all looked familiar, too. So many police call-outs end up with the Fire Brigade or Ambulance Service called in, it was inevitable that we would have come across each other at some time.

'Okay, Rich,' one of the paramedics said. 'You were going to get great care anyway. But now you're going to get the best. We look after our own here in Napa.'

Amen to that.

I tried to say it out loud but nothing happened. My mouth didn't open and my tongue didn't move. The paramedic kneeling in front of me saw the panic in my eyes.

'You're going to be okay, Rich. I just need to check a few things.'

I watched as he grabbed a black band and hand pump from his medical kit. I'd used a blood-pressure cuff dozens of times myself, so I didn't resist when he wrapped it tightly around my left arm. The familiar sound of the Velcro fastener followed, then the urgent constriction on my biceps as the guy inflated the cuff. All the while he questioned Lili, asking her how long I'd been like this.

'He started complaining of dizziness at about eight,' she said.

'Was he able to talk?'

'He was able to do everything when I left the house.'

'When was that?'

'Thirty minutes ago.'

Thirty minutes? Is it possible to get from feeling a bit light-headed to unable to control my own jaw in that time?

Obviously it was.

Lili and the paramedics continued talking while they took my pulse and ran a couple of other tests. I realised that I'd never heard my wife talking like this before. She sounded like me when I used to be the first responder at murder scenes and was the only sane voice in the room until back-up arrived. You can worry about the details and your own feelings when you finish your shift. But in that moment you have to be 100 per cent professional. You see only your work and what has to be done. You turn off all emotion, all normal human reactions, and just ask the questions that need to be asked, do the things that need to be done. I'd managed the switch from human to professional for twenty-five years.

And now, I realised with pride, Lili could do it too.

Lili isn't in professional mode now. She's questioning her own behaviour. Was there anything she could have done, any clues she should have spotted? After all, she's a nurse. She has two decades' medical experience. The other voice assures her she did nothing wrong.

'But what if I'd been at work when Rich first called?' Lili persists. 'That time could have made a difference.'

'How long was it before you called him back?'

'Two minutes. Maybe three.'

'Then how could that have made a difference?'

Lili falls silent. Then she says, 'I knew there was something wrong as soon as I got the message from the receptionist.'

'What did she say?'

'She asked me, "Has he been drinking?" I think she was joking. But she couldn't understand a word Rich had said. He'd lost control of his voice even then.'

So that explains why she couldn't understand me! It wasn't her language problem; it was my speech problem.

'What about when you called him?'

'He was exactly the same. But I never thought it was a stroke. I just knew I had to dial 911 and get back home as quickly as I could.'

My control over my body was coming and going. Obviously, when I'd rung Lili's office I'd sounded like a man on the wrong end of a weekend pub-crawl. Yet, when she'd arrived back home, I'd managed to spit out, 'I think I'm having a stroke!' as clear as day. And

I'd propped myself up in the doorway for the three or four minutes it took for the cavalry to arrive before losing all the strength
in my legs the moment they did.

I could still *feel*, though. The tightness of the cuff on my arm
was really biting now. The pressure of the second paramedic's finger
on my neck as he took my pulse hurt, too. The weight of my own
hand resting on my thigh was no different from how it would have
been the day before. But feeling and control are two different things.
The hand that weighed heavily on my leg felt like it belonged to a
stranger. I could see the paramedic's hands on it, I could feel his fingers, but I couldn't move it. Not one inch. Not for one second.

That was when I realised what I was feeling above everything
else.

Fear.

I was terrified. No one had contradicted my diagnosis. I really
was having a stroke. I'd personally known only one stroke victim –
my grandma on my mother's side. It hadn't killed her, but she was
disabled for the rest of her life.

Is that what's going to happen to me?

Despite the assurance that I was about to receive the best treatment, I could see the stress on the faces of the four men who were
committed to helping me. I'd been in enough similar situations to
recognise when first responders were trying to put on a brave face.

Hell, I've done it enough times myself.

No paramedic will tell a hit-and-run victim that he's going to
die, even if the guy's organs are scattered across the road. No fire-
fighter is going to tell a woman she's disfigured, no matter how
bad it looks at the scene. So I knew the answer, even though I
couldn't force the question out of my mouth.

'You're going to be fine, Rich. Everything's fine.'

That scared me even more.

CHAPTER THREE

You're in the Best Place Now

Faces.

One on each side of the bed, staring down into my eyes. I wonder how long they've been there. I keep drifting off. They must have been waiting until I woke up.

Let's get it over with, then. I'm ready. Tell me what happened – and don't worry about pulling any punches. I was a cop for twenty-five years. I've seen things you wouldn't believe. I can take it.

Talk to me.

I'm ready.

Talk to me. Damn it, don't just stand there. Talk to me, someone. Tell me what is going on!

When things started going seriously wrong, I had one thought in my mind.

I just want my Lili.

All I could think of was getting her back to the house so she could sort it out. That's how close we were.

From the moment I'd set eyes on her across the gym floor, I'd been smitten. Seeing a stunning woman lifting serious weights was not an everyday occurrence, even in a Californian gym. She was about five foot three, with dark-brown hair, brown skin, brown eyes, a really wide smile whenever she saw someone she knew – and tattoos. There was a whole sleeve of them on one arm.

I'd been married three times already, but I had no hesitation in making the walk up the aisle again in 2006 with this woman who was eight years my junior. To this day, neither of us has uttered as much as a single cross word in the other's direction.

Fast-forward three years and whatever was happening to me that Wednesday morning, I felt that Lili would be able to take care of it. That's an unreasonable amount of pressure to put on another person, but it was what I was thinking. She was already so special to me, but at that moment in time she was everything.

Which was why the next sixty minutes were so hard to take.

I'd been so impressed with the way her professional side had kicked in. She'd stood aside, flicked into nurse mode and answered the paramedics' questions with admirable detachment and calmness. Another partner would have been in hysterics, but Lili held it together for my sake.

When the paramedics had finished their checks for vital signs, the EMTs took over.

'Rich, can you walk to the door?' one said.

I nodded.

Of course I can walk to the door.

But first I had to get up, and that, I realised, was not going to happen without assistance.

I think Lili saw the pain in my eyes first.

'He needs help,' she said.

'No problem.'

The EMTs hoisted me up, leveraged me under the arms again, and we were soon on the move. I thought once I was up I'd be okay, that I would be able to make the fifteen feet to the front porch alone. But I had nothing. My legs wouldn't move. They couldn't even support my weight.

Confusion came first.

I didn't understand. Doesn't a stroke affect only one side? My grandma lost all the feeling on her left side, but her right side remained normal. Instinctively, I focused all my concentration on my right foot. If I had to hop through the door I would do it. Anything to get a bit of dignity back. A bit of control over my own body.

I channelled everything I had into that foot, but it didn't move. I realised I was just staring at it. In disbelief, in anger. In downright bewilderment. No one teaches you how to move your legs. It's not like taking driving lessons or learning to cook. It's not like the information I used to rattle off in classes for the attentive sponges to soak up. No one is told how to walk. I realised then how little I knew about my own body. It's not like there are any buttons or levers, computers or 'on' switches. I literally had no idea how to make my right leg move.

The confusion turned into panic.

What is happening to me?

The EMTs looked at me, then at each other. Their grip never wavered. But what if it did? What if they thought I could stand up on my own?

I'm six foot two. That's a long way from my face to the ground. I'd seen guys fall from lower heights and break arms, legs, even necks. I could worry later about whatever was happening to me. At that moment I was just terrified they would let go.

'It's okay, Rich, we've got you,' the guy on my left said.

I nodded at him and tried to say 'thanks'. But, like my legs, my tongue had gone on strike. I couldn't even open my mouth.

How was that possible? I'd spoken to Lili just five minutes earlier. How could I not even thank these men who were trying to help me? How can you forget how to speak?

It was time to go. The EMTs started moving towards the door and I felt my feet dragging limply against the hardwood floor. I could feel the contact with every stride but I couldn't control anything. I was a puppet, but instead of strings I was held up by the strong arms of the Ambulance Service. This was even worse than not being able to speak. My feet were dead weights. Useless.

It was the lowest point of my life.

What is wrong with these people? They look like doctors but they're acting like clowns. They're even talking to each other now, across me, as though I'm not here. Why would they do that? Why would they ignore me? They need to work on their bedside manner.

And aren't they sweating, wearing so many clothes?

The sky had never been bluer. The breeze on my face was warm. The hum of traffic was steady. But I wasn't out on my motorbike. I was face up, strapped to the gurney, being pushed along the concrete drive by four men in a hurry.

Their shoulders and heads obscured a lot of the view. I couldn't make out any flowers or the lawn. I couldn't even see Lili. Only when the high branches of our old oak sprawled into view did I realise we'd reached the road.

I knew the drill from here. The gurney would be wheeled into the road, behind the ambulance's open rear doors. It would be pushed flush to the flat bed, its front wheels would collapse as the men around me took the strain, and then they would slide me into the back. One of the EMTs would drive, the other would sit with me in the back. Maybe one of the paramedics would ride in the ambulance as well. I didn't care whether he came along or not. The only person I really wanted at my side was my wife.

The loading went exactly as I predicted. Even with the EMT and a paramedic on board there was still room for one more.

'You're welcome to travel with us,' the guy who'd recognised me said to Lili.

She was out of my eye line but I could hear her words.

'You know what?' she said. 'I need to lock the house and make arrangements at Rich's work. I'll follow in my car.'

I heard every word, but it took a few seconds to process their meaning.

You're not coming with me?

I shouted it.

Or at least I tried to shout it. Still nothing worked. I couldn't even produce a garbled noise. How could I make my wife understand that I needed her with me?

Suddenly a new shadow was cast over me and I realised it was Lili climbing into the ambulance. She'd heard me somehow. She'd got the message. Then she told me she'd see me soon, kissed my head and climbed back out to lock the house.

She was still in full-on nurse mode and for that second I hated her for it. As the ambulance doors closed, I couldn't believe she'd left me. I knew her reasons. I'd heard her say them. She was just doing her job and letting the professionals do theirs. But everything I'd admired about her in the house a few minutes earlier – her pragmatism, her logic, her calmness – I now resented.

This isn't the time for efficiency, Lili. It's the time to be my wife!

How long have I been asleep?

The faces have gone. I listen to the buzz of the machines lined up on my right-hand side. I watch my chest rise and fall in time with the sound of mechanical bellows pumping the air. For a while it's all I can see and all I can hear. Then I realise there is nothing else. No other sounds from the corridor or from my room. The TV is turned down to almost inaudible. I can't even hear any noise from outside the window.

And I definitely can't hear Lili.

Where is she? She's always here. How am I supposed to get through this without her?

The piercing shrill of the siren filled the rear of the ambulance as we tore through the morning Napa traffic. I knew the light sequence that would be accompanying it. The gurney straps across my chest kept me in place as the ambulance took the curves. I guessed we were heading to the Queen of the Valley Medical Center. At this speed it wouldn't take very long.

It wasn't just the vehicle that was moving quickly. The EMT and paramedic were busily scrabbling around in drawers and medicine boxes, like passers-by trying to catch notes spewing from a faulty ATM. Both were talking – although not to each other. The EMT was shouting into a phone warning someone that he was on his way with a patient who wasn't looking too good. It took me a few seconds to appreciate he was talking about me. On the plus side, I learned that I was right about our destination.

The paramedic was even more energetic. He maintained a running commentary of everything he did, throwing in the occasional question to me, but never leaving time for an answer. He knew as well as I did that answering was impossible. He also knew that any reply would be irrelevant. His plan was simply to keep me alert, to monitor my every breath and make sure I stayed conscious. It was standard procedure, something I'd witnessed hundreds of times.

Suddenly he picked up my left arm and rolled up my shirt-sleeve from my wrist. A second later he was dabbing something on the back of my hand. Moments after that there was a jolting pain. I instinctively tried to withdraw my left arm and fight him off with my right. My left hand didn't budge, but it was only the straps across my chest that stopped my right arm flying into his face. Control of it seemed to have returned as inexplicably as it had disappeared.

Maybe I'm over the worst, I thought, anxious for the chance to stand on my own two feet again. *Maybe it's all been a bad dream.*

The paramedic brought me back to reality.

'That's the IV unit connected,' he explained, to me or his colleague, I couldn't tell.

'We're pulling into the Queen of the Valley now,' the EMT announced. 'They should be expecting us.' Then, looking directly at me for the first time since we'd set off, he added, 'You're in the best place now, Rich. Godspeed.'

CHAPTER FOUR

Shutting Down

'I don't know what I was thinking. How long does it take to lock up a house?'

I've never heard Lili so upset. That, in turn, makes me sad. Especially as she's talking to me.

'The second they closed the ambulance doors I knew I'd made a mistake. But by then it was too late.'

She's standing by the window with her back to me. She can't even bear to face me.

'What if something had happened on the journey? What if . . .'

Then there's silence. She can't finish her sentence. She's too cut up.

I want to tell her there's no need to apologise. I want to tell her I understand – even though I don't – and that she shouldn't worry. But most of all I want to thank her for talking to me like I'm a real person and not treating me like some shop dummy in pyjamas. Everyone else talks about me rather than to me. It's such a privilege to be acknowledged for once, even if Lili can't bring herself to look at me.

'What if he never made it?' she continues, finally.

Hang on. He? Who are you talking about, Lili? Who are you talking to?

Then she half turns and I see the cocked angle of her head, the cupped shape of her hand and the shadow of a small, black mobile phone pressed to her ear.

Oh. You're not talking to me at all, are you? The pauses weren't you catching your breath, too choked to speak. You were listening to someone else. Someone you can hear. Someone you know exists.

I'm the invisible man to you, too.

I'd followed enough ambulances to the Queen of the Valley – or 'The Queen' as its staff called it – to recognise the route we had taken. Even in the back of an ambulance, eyes fixed firmly on the ceiling, I could sense where we were throughout the journey. The longest stretch was along St Helena's Highway. Then we had to come off onto Trancas Street. And finally, when the ambulance swung a sharp left and killed its speed, I knew we'd arrived.

For most admissions, that's where you stop. But ambulances get to cut around to the left of the large, sprawling building and park directly outside the Emergency Room. Not only can they unload patients directly into the heart of the building, they can do so uninterrupted by the citizens clogging up the administration area on Trancas Street itself.

The back doors opened and daylight flooded in. My attendants leapt out, gathering leads and bags with them. Two porters were waiting and didn't need to ask for information.

'He's stable,' my paramedic called out. 'But he's shutting down. Fast.'

I was.

There had been moments during the short journey when I'd felt back in control of my limbs. I could wiggle the fingers on my right hand and twitch my toes just by looking at them.

But that seemed like an age ago now.

As we'd hit Trancas Street I wasn't even thinking about the destination. I was only thinking about my own body. About myself. About what was happening to me.

It started with my left foot. One minute I could move my toes; the next they'd gone. My left leg followed, then my right foot, then that leg. My left arm had been lost from the start but now my right joined it. It was like my entire body was powering down. I could still feel everything – the bumpy ride, the coarse straps across my chest, the IV tube in my hand – but I couldn't react. I couldn't control anything. I'd seen movies where the lights turned out across a city, block by block. That was exactly how I felt. Limb by limb – block by block – the lights went out.

Inch by inch, nothingness spread over my body.

As the gurney was being lowered onto the smooth pavement outside the Emergency Room I tried to raise my head to look for Lili. It didn't budge. It stayed fixed, glued almost, on the hard, padded headrest.

I can't even turn my head.

And I still had no idea where Lili was.

Anyone who has ever seen an episode of *ER* will know exactly what happened next. The porters grabbed the gurney and virtually ran me into the building. Up ramps, through swing doors, all at full speed. I knew why they were in such a hurry. My knowledge of strokes was limited, but I did know that the sooner you are diagnosed, the greater are your chances of recovery. It had been less than an hour since I'd called Lili at the hospice, so at least that was in my favour.

But what if I had a different problem? What if it was something worse? So far the only person who had even mentioned the word 'stroke' had been me.

And what do I know?

Lili. On her phone? Or talking to someone behind me? I can't tell this time. She's certainly animated, though. Beating herself up again.

'They wouldn't even let me in – and I used to work here, can you believe that?'

She pauses. Listening to someone's reply on her mobile or fighting back her own emotions? I can't tell.

'They wouldn't let me in because they didn't know who I was. Ambulances arriving at the Queen of the Valley go in one entrance. People like me – people who have to park a car – have to come in the main entrance. It's on the other side of the building. And could I get them to let me through? No.'

Don't be so hard on yourself, Lili.

'I had to stand in line, along with all the people trying to get treatment. I couldn't even push to the front because everyone in that room had an emergency of their own. And there was nothing wrong with me, so how could I justify pushing in front of a kid with blood pouring out of his leg or the pregnant mom who looked fit to pop?'

It doesn't matter, my darling.

'Eventually I did get to the front. The receptionist took my details, looked at her computer and told me no one with Rich's name had been admitted! "Are you sure he came to this hospital?" Of course I was sure, I followed the ambulance! But she wouldn't take it. It was only when I suggested he maybe wasn't on her system yet that she finally started to believe me. She picked up her phone and made a call to the Emergency Room. Why she couldn't have done that right away I don't know. When she hung up she smiled.

'"Your husband has been admitted. He's being seen to right now. If you'd like to take a seat someone will update you when they have information."

'Update me? I told her, "I don't want to be updated. I want to be with him!"'

It kills me to hear this. Lili has told me that people being treated in hospital rarely realise the pain their loved ones go through or the hurdles they have to jump just to get some information. Well, I don't have that luxury. I can hear the pain and frustration in my wife's voice. The closest I've been to that situation was when my kids were born. You feel like you're banging your head against a brick wall, and for what? A bit of information. That was all I wanted back then and that's all Lili wants now.

I know medics have only one priority – to save lives – so customer care isn't high on their agenda. But maybe it should be. That would have saved Lili a lot of unnecessary suffering when I was admitted. And that, in turn, would have saved me a lot, too. Even as I was taken into the Emergency Room and examined by a specialist stroke doctor, all I could think was, Where's Lili?

Where's my wife?

The paramedics had disappeared. The EMTs had gone, too, taking their gurney with them, the second I'd been transferred to a hospital trolley. I wished I could have thanked them.

I wouldn't be here without them.

But where was 'here'? I was in a large room full of medical equipment and an examination table. In front of me stood a woman and two men. They were all dressed in white. The first to speak looked older than the others. He had white hair, glasses and authority written all over him. I guessed he was in charge. Maybe he could tell me what was going on with my body – and where my wife was.

'I'm sending you for a CAT scan, Richard,' he said. 'Do you understand?'

'I do.'

Did I just speak?

Out of nowhere I seemed to have regained control of my tongue. I hadn't felt it come back, it was just suddenly there. The words sounded pretty slurred, but from the look on the doctor's face, he could make them out. And from the way he looked at his colleagues, he was as surprised as I was.

'As soon as we do the scan we'll know what we're facing,' he explained.

I tried to ask about Lili but this time nothing came out. How could my mouth work once and then be useless thirty seconds later? Had I imagined speaking before? Was that it?

Two porters grabbed my trolley and spun me round. But before we went anywhere they started unbuttoning, unzipping and unfastening my clothes. They could have warned me. Admirable efficiency came at the expense of finesse. It took them less than two minutes to get me completely naked and then wrapped inside a traditional hospital gown. Clark Kent couldn't have changed into Superman any quicker. But at least his costume wasn't made of paper. Mine itched from the moment it touched my skin. And the noise! The gown crinkled and rustled with every nudge of the trolley. I should have had more pressing concerns, but that noise seemed to fill my brain. For a couple of minutes, it was all I could think about.

The second I was decent, the porters grabbed the trolley again and headed for the door. The scanning department was down in the basement, so we had some ground to cover.

'I just burst into tears. I'm a grown woman and I'm a nurse, for God's sake, but that was all I could come up with. I just pictured Rich alone somewhere in that huge hospital, not knowing what was happening to him and thinking I'd abandoned him.'

Lili is taking this far too personally, and I wish I could say something to reassure her. But she's discussing it with someone else, not me.

You can tell me anything, Lili. I'm only over here.

'Finally they took pity on me. Someone came out and found me and said that Rich was being taken for a scan. If I was lucky, I'd get there in time to watch.'

I'm laughing now, at least inside. Luck didn't enter into it – she's the fittest, fastest person I know. I remember the look on her face when she arrived. So scared for me but not a hair out of place. No one would have guessed she'd just sprinted right across the campus.

But I was ecstatic she did.

I'd faced death, directly or indirectly, most of my working life. It was as much a part of the job as wearing the badge or pulling on the uniform. I took it in my stride every day that I holstered my weapon and climbed into my patrol car. And I'd been lucky. I'd managed to come through a quarter of a century in law enforcement facing murderers, gang-runners and drug-fuelled maniacs without a scratch. But I could still identify danger when I saw it, and it still scared me. Being scared was another part of the job, and every time I met someone who told me he was never afraid I knew I was in the presence of a liar – or a liability. Fear is a natural part of every experienced police officer's daily life, but I learned a few little mental tricks to keep it in check.

As I entered the trauma room, I wished I could have remembered just one of them.

Again, the TV comparisons hit me instantly. It was like being wheeled onto the set of *Star Trek* or some other futuristic adventure. Silver, steel and chrome were the dominant colours. Detergent was the overpowering aroma. And uncertainty was in the air, among the doctors at least. I was beyond uncertain. I was terrified of what was happening to me.

But also of what I was about to undergo.

I couldn't even turn my head to acknowledge the doctor who was explaining the CAT scan to me. By shifting my eyes to the extreme right I could just make out the top of his head. He didn't seem to care whether I could hear him or not. The main priority was obviously to get the process under way. In hindsight, I'm grateful to him for that. At the time, though, I felt like a minor part in his smooth operation.

The CAT – computer-assisted tomography – scanner, I was told, produces cross-sectional X-ray images of the whole body. Whatever was wrong with me, it would find it. Bugs, growths, afflictions, it would – *should* – pinpoint them all.

That was the theory. But I was the one who had to deal with the practice. And, far from a sleek piece of equipment in a sci-fi medical bay, the scanner looked like a giant doughnut and sounded like a malfunctioning microwave. It was confusing, baffling, terrifying. I knew it was designed to help me, but it looked like something from a mad scientist's laboratory. Which made me the lab rat.

The only way I was going to get through this was knowing Lili was there.

And she was.

She'd arrived as we'd left the Emergency Room. She'd flung herself on me even as we sped down the long, bleak corridor, and told me she was sorry it had taken so long to get there. I'd smiled. In my head at least. I don't know what my mouth did. It didn't feel like it was doing much at all.

'It's okay,' I wanted to say. But my voice wasn't working either.

Come on, Marsh, you just spoke to the doctor – you can talk to your own wife!

Coming and going, controlling and not controlling, speaking and not speaking – the inconsistency was killing me. But it was also a distraction. When I arrived for the scan, the experience charged at me like a bull. The doctor had told me what to expect, but I hadn't taken it in. Now there was no choice.

The two porters lifted me from the trolley and onto what looked like a game show conveyor belt. I was told it would take me inside the giant doughnut, where I'd be photographed internally. That all sounded fine. Nothing to worry about.

Until I saw the porters running for cover.

They joined the doctor, Lili and everyone else behind a wall on the other side of the room. There was no getting away from it – I was about to undergo something dangerous. Something so dangerous that it was a threat to innocent bystanders like my wife and the doctors.

But then an even more disturbing thought entered my mind. If they were willing to subject me to *this* threat, how dangerous was the predicament that had brought me here?

'You have to keep perfectly still,' the lab technician instructed me.

I can't do anything else.

Thought, rather than said. My tongue was now superglued to the back of my mouth. In fact, it was feeling heavier than ever. I hadn't noticed until I'd tried to use it.

Panic.

You take so many things for granted. I've done so all my life. But lying there, about to be fed into a toxic luggage carousel, I was suddenly aware of the inertia at the back of my throat. I couldn't move my legs, my arms were dead to me and my head felt like a hundredweight rock. But it was inside – in my mouth – where I couldn't cope. I could feel my tongue, heavy and wide, but more than that I could feel my saliva pressing against it. I don't think I'd ever thought of my own saliva in sixty years. But there I was, not only aware of it for the first time, but feeling it building up against my tongue. Pushing, pressurising, filling my mouth.

Biology had never been my strongest subject at school, but my CSI work – for the police and Napa High School – had filled my head with a lot of information. And I knew that a surfeit of liquid in the mouth, if unchecked – or unswallowed – would lead to only one result.

Death. By drowning.

Thankfully, my throat was still working. I could feel myself gulping, funnelling the spittle that had built up in my mouth to safety. But, I was chastened to realise, it was happening on autopilot. I was not even in control of that.

I tried to find a positive. *Be grateful your body knows what it's doing.*

But did it? If the ability to tell my wife I loved her – or to walk, stand or smile – had vanished, how could I be sure my capacity to swallow a mouthful of spit would hang around much longer?

I'm going to die …

There was a final shove and I was under the lights. Anyone who has spent ten minutes in a solarium would have been familiar with the sensation. But I wasn't. I felt like a corn cob waiting to be blasted.

There was a click and a whirr, then the lights came on. Something was happening. I was being examined. Tested. Investigated by the sliding bar above my head. A giant comb passed above me, beaming light down, highlighting every inch of my body. The gown lit up. Every crinkle, every fold, was under the spotlight. Colours disappeared. Only white remained.

I closed my eyes and prayed I'd have the ability to open them by the time it was over.

CHAPTER FIVE

Look at His Eyes

Why do I keep falling asleep? No wonder everyone is treating me like they can't see me. They must think I'm constantly asleep. They probably don't want to wake me.

But I'm not asleep. If I were, I wouldn't be able to hear that rustling sound. Where is it coming from? It sounds like paper fluttering in a breeze. Is there a fan on in here, or aircon? There can't be, it's too hot. Don't tell me they've put the heating on. In May? In California? That's just ridiculous. How am I supposed to recover when it's too hot to think?

'Now for the anatomy lesson.'

We were back in the trauma room. The same doctor I'd seen before was standing in front of me. His eyes flicked between mine and Lili's, then towards another man. He was introduced as a neurologist. It was his job, the doctor said, to explain what they'd learned in the basement.

'We've got the results of the CAT scan,' the neurologist began, 'and they mostly confirm what we thought. Rich, you've had a stroke. A very large one.' He paused. 'Now, a lot of people make a full recovery from strokes. But, I have to warn you, most of those strokes are nothing like yours.'

'What's the difference?' Lili asked.

I wanted to know as well, but doubted I'd understand the explanation. I felt my CSI knowledge was about to be severely tested.

'Strokes are caused by a lack of oxygen to the brain,' the neurologist explained. 'There are two ways this can happen. Most strokes are caused by a clot, or thrombus. This is called an ischemic stroke. The other type is a haemorrhagic stroke, where an artery bursts and floods the brain with blood.'

So far, so good.

'According to our scan, you have had an ischemic stroke.'

Great. So I'm in the majority, then. I've had the common type. They'll know how to deal with it.

'So he has a blood clot?' Lili asked, looking for confirmation.

The doctor nodded.

'But how?' Lili asked. 'I thought strokes only affected alcoholics and stressed people. Rich is so fit. He eats all the right things – he grows most of them in our garden. He works out. He's never taken a day off work in his life. He's not even that old! How is this possible?'

I could see the fear in her eyes. The neurologist saw it, too. I couldn't make out what his eyes were saying, though. I just heard his words.

'I'm afraid it's got nothing to do with Rich's lifestyle,' he said finally.

'What do you mean?'

Give him a chance to explain, Lili!

'Clots can be caused by a trauma to the head, or elsewhere in the body. Or by a sedentary lifestyle. Sitting still for too long on a long-haul flight can also cause deep-vein thrombosis – another name for a blood clot. At this stage, we don't know what caused Rich's clot. But we do know what happened next.

'There are three arteries leading up to the brain,' he continued. 'On each side you have a carotid artery, feeding the left and right sides of the brain, respectively. A stroke in this area usually causes paralysis down one side of the body or the other.'

That's not what I've got.

He looked directly at me. 'That's not what you've got, Richard,' he said. 'Unfortunately.'

That sounds ominous.

He paused again. I guessed to choose his words carefully. I thought I even saw him cast a glance at the other doctor. What was he looking for? Moral support? That wouldn't be a good sign. I tried to convince myself I'd imagined it.

'In very few cases, no more than ten per cent of all strokes, people can get a clot in the central – or basilar – artery,' he eventually continued. 'This artery connects directly to the brain stem. However, this does not always lead to a stroke. The basilar has two minor arteries that feed into it. A clot in one of these will slow down your blood supply but the other channel should be able to cope.'

He was building to the meat of the matter now, I could feel it.

'Unfortunately, Richard, our scan has shown that you do not have two functioning minor arteries. One of yours is a dead end; it does not lead anywhere. And, because your clot is in the other one, there is nowhere for the blood to go.'

'Why hasn't this affected him before?' Lili asked, sounding as professional as ever.

'There's no reason why it should have affected his life. A surprising number of people have this condition and go through life without it ever being an issue.'

'Are you saying he was born like this?'

'Almost certainly. It's only come to light now because of the clot.'

Listening to this biology lesson was like being back at high school. Except I was no longer the teacher – I was the student, and a poor one at that. Fortunately for me, Lili was keeping up.

'Can you operate?' she asked. 'Can you cut it out?'

Good girl. She's still in nurse mode, cutting to the chase.

'Unfortunately, that's where it gets tricky.'

This doesn't sound good.

'Damage in the basilar area is usually not survivable. Because of that, the risk of operating here is too great.'

'There must be something you can do,' Lili said. Her 'on duty' voice had disappeared. Suddenly she was sounding like my wife again.

Another bad sign …

The neurologist looked at me.

'Well, there is a drug that could help,' he said. 'It's a type of TPA – tissue plasminogen activator. Its name is Activase, but we call it the "clot buster" because that's essentially what it does.'

It worked, he explained, by diffusing the clot. It had to be administered within three hours of the stroke occurring, but it had the potential side-effect of making the blood too thin.

The neurologist addressed me directly: 'Do you understand what I'm saying, Richard?' he asked.

I nodded.

'Yes,' I croaked, and we were all surprised when the word – or something close to it – came out. I hadn't been able to say anything for so long. When had that ability returned?

'And do you want to go ahead with the clot buster?'

I tried to say 'yes' again, but this time nothing happened. The power of speech had left me as briskly as it had returned. But at least I was still able to nod. The effort left me breathless, but I got my point across.

Immediately, the neurologist started moving. Time, he said, was against us. We were still within the three-hour window, but it was closing. Fast.

Are they saying I'm going to die?

It certainly sounds like it. 'Not survivable,' the neurologist said. 'Inoperable' – I think he said that, too. And 'less than ten per cent' means this type of stroke is rare, which can't be good.

Did he mention what usually happens to the victims? I don't think he did. I wonder why not. Has he got something to hide?

Then I remember something about 'three hours'. How long has it been since I collapsed at home? The scan took about forty-five minutes. How many minutes do I have left?

We're against the clock. I can almost hear it ticking. I'm relying on this man, this neurologist – this stranger – to save my life. He's the one rushing around. There's nothing I can do to help.

I guess I'm going to have to get used to that feeling. I'm helpless.

And that's not all. My breathing is so laboured and my mouth is filling with my own spittle again. There's nothing I can do about it. I've forgotten how to swallow.

I need to tell the doctor. But now nothing is working. I can't make a sound.

The neurologist wasn't the only person on the go. Even as he ran from the room – I guessed to fetch some vital piece of equipment – the original doctor was scurrying around me. He called a nurse over.

'Listen to Richard's breathing,' he said. 'He's struggling to manage his secretions.'

I'm what?

The nurse nodded. 'He's struggling to get air,' she said. 'I think the diaphragm is shutting down.'

'Yes,' the doctor agreed, looking straight at me this time. 'I'm afraid we're going to have to intubate.'

I didn't know what that meant. Lili did, of course, and the concern was etched across her face. Unlike with the clot buster, I clearly wasn't being given a choice.

The doors flew open and the neurologist burst back in. He went straight over to my IV stand and replaced the bag with another he'd brought with him.

'This is the clot buster, Richard,' he said. 'We need to give it time to work but hopefully it will do the trick.'

I knew what he was saying was important, but I was only half listening. My more immediate concern was: *What the hell does 'intubate' mean?*

I don't know what 'manage his secretions' means, either. Do they mean the stuff being produced by my mouth? Do they mean my spittle? Have they noticed I'm finding it hard to swallow? If they have, why don't they just say that?

And what's this about my diaphragm? Is that even possible? Can a stroke shut down your organs? It's meant to affect your left or right side, your arms, your legs, your face, isn't it? Not your insides. But if my diaphragm is starting to fail, what else might shut down? If your organs stop working, you die, right?

I'm more worried than ever now. Worried that everything I think I know about strokes is wrong. Worried that this thing has been inside me from birth, ticking away like a time-bomb. Or a like a sleeper agent, waiting for the moment to strike.

So why now? Why has it decided to get me today? Have I done something wrong?

I like logic. I like consequences. I like cause and effect. I like things to happen for a reason. But there's no reason here. It's so random. And that's unfair. It's not a word I use often, but there's no choice. It's unfair.

I'm close to losing it. The pool in my mouth is growing by the second. I focus all my concentration on swallowing, trying to make the saliva slip down my throat and away to safety.

But nothing's moving. Not my tongue, not my throat, not the liquid in my mouth.

I try to rationalise it. Tell myself it's probably just a spoonful of spittle. A teaspoon at that. But the longer it stays there, the larger it feels. Now it's a soup spoon. Now it's a dessert spoon. Now it's a tablespoon.

I'm desperate to shift it, but it's not budging. Not even a trickle disappears down my throat. The more I try, the worse it gets.

Suddenly I picture myself in a room filling with water. It's pouring in from somewhere, and fast. At the moment it's level with my waist. But it's rising. I'm sliding further and further underwater.

I try to swallow again. Nothing.

The water's at my chest. I'm getting anxious. I can breathe at the moment, but for how much longer?

The water is at my shoulders. It lifts me and I'm treading water. I tilt my head back to keep my mouth above the water line. I'm looking at the ceiling, which is getting closer. I'm lying on my back now, floating. I can still breathe – but only just.

Any second now my face will touch the hard, white surface of the ceiling. Then there'll be nowhere to go.

My body is trapped, pinned to ceiling, as the liquid that I've taken for granted all my life fills my mouth, my throat, my nose.

I'm drowning. My own body is killing me.

'Look at his eyes!' Lili was agitated. 'What's happening?'

I'd never felt anything like it before. Was the blood clot

shutting down my brain as well? I could have sworn I was peering out from the inside of a fish tank, banging on the glass, trying to escape. I had no oxygen tank, no snorkel. Just a single mouthful of breath that was fast running out.

The more I pounded on the wall of the tank, the more I could feel the burning in my lungs. I didn't know how much longer I could last.

All I could think about was Lili's anxious face. That told me I wasn't imagining it. Not all of it, anyway. I really was in trouble.

The frenetic activity of the medical team confirmed my worst fears. I'd been in the eye of the storm many times before, so I knew what an emergency looked like. So did the neurologist. I watched him stand back to allow the nurse and the other doctor through to me.

I was still banging on the glass of the fish tank as the doctor approached. Then I felt my arm being lifted and the skin rubbed. This time I knew they were preparing it for a needle, so I looked across to Lili. I didn't need to see the needle piercing my skin. Unfortunately, I couldn't avert my ears, so I heard exactly how crucial it was for them to get it into me – *now!*

Then everything went black.

CHAPTER SIX

Work the Clues

'The only way I can describe it is if you've ever seen a movie where some-one's drowning. It was just like that. His eyes were wide open. They were popping out on stalks. He couldn't say anything or move anything but I could tell he was scared as hell. He was terrified he was running out of air.'

Lili's talking to someone but she's outside my field of vision. Maybe she's on the phone again. I want to tell her she's spot on. I was terrified. I was running out of air.

But I have no idea what happened next. No idea what they did to me or where they took me.

The taste of rubber.

I recognised that. Maybe I wasn't actually tasting it, though. How would I know what rubber tasted like? But I knew the smell and I knew the texture. There was no doubt in my mind that there was rubber near me somewhere.

My head was throbbing. But why?

The last thing I remembered was ...

The drowning.

It came back to me like a lightning bolt. I hadn't been able to breathe. My mouth had filled with saliva and I couldn't swallow. My tongue had felt like a one-ton weight and I couldn't move it out of the way. Just remembering that brought the cold sweat of fear back to me. But I wasn't drowning now, was I?

I couldn't recall ever trying to focus on the back of my own throat before, but I was doing so now.

Where was the pool of spittle?

It had vanished. But something else was in its place. I was amazed it had taken me so long to notice it. My God, it was uncomfortable. And, in its own way, it was even more terrifying than the saliva had been.

That was the first of several startling realisations.

My mouth was open – the thing inside was so large that there was no other option – my jaw ached and my throat was on fire.

There's something down there as well.

The sensation of drowning – feeling short of breath and panicking as my lungs struggled for oxygen – was still fresh in my memory, but now I had the opposite problem. Air was all around me, closing in on me, crushing me, like in a rubbish dumper. It was squeezing me to death.

I felt claustrophobic.

It's like being buried alive.

An image of Uma Thurman in *Kill Bill* came to mind. Michael Madsen had trapped her in a coffin. Buried her alive. Is there a worse way to go? I couldn't think of one. I knew at that moment I was going to die. Right there and then. What other outcome could there be?

Somehow, though, I managed to get a grip. Uma Thurman had escaped, so why couldn't I? I had to work it through, work it out.

First, I concluded that I wasn't underground after all. The sensation of being buried alive must have been caused by the thing in my mouth. It had to be some sort of pipe. What else could hurt in so many places at once? I felt it touching my teeth, in my mouth and down the back of my throat. How had this happened? Who had subjected me to this torture? Medical centres were meant to help you, not hurt you. And make no mistake, this hurt like hell. It was like having a burning flame forced down your throat. Every single breath made me want to gag. Every single inhalation made me want to scream in agony.

But I couldn't gag. I couldn't scream. In fact, I couldn't do anything.

That was the second realisation.

I was acutely aware of the intense, inferno-like sensation in my mouth and throat, but I couldn't do anything about it. I couldn't lick my lips. I couldn't move my tongue. I couldn't even move my neck to check whether anything was hanging out of my mouth. My head was frozen, immobile, stuck.

This is scary.

I wondered what else couldn't I do, which sent a chill running through me. I felt it, but even then my body didn't budge. There was no shudder. No shiver. Was I imagining all of this? How could I feel so much and control so little?

I felt like a wrestler with every limb pinned to the canvas by my opponent. There was literally nothing I could do.

I remembered the doctor taking hold of my arm in the trauma room and preparing it for an injection. When had that been? What had happened afterwards? What had he pumped into me?

Gingerly, I opened my eyes.

Or did I? By now I'd been awake for a few minutes. On a

normal day, my eyes would have sprung open the second I left sleep behind, either instinctively or through a conscious decision on my part. But this was not a normal day, and the lids had stayed glued shut even while I panicked about being buried alive. Now, finally, they'd opened, but I didn't really know why.

Did I make them do that or did they do it of their accord?

I needed to find out. I had to discover whether I still had the power to control my own eyelids.

I tried to close them again. Nothing happened. I tried to blink. Still nothing. I felt the heat of panic rising in my body again, but that was something I *could* control. At least in part. I told myself there was no point worrying about blinking now. I just had to be grateful that I could still see. I figured it was better to be trapped in the light than in the dark.

As the panic subsided I realised I was looking forwards – not upwards, not at the ceiling. My head was at an angle. Perhaps it was resting on a pillow. It felt soft on the back of my head, but not *soft* soft. Not like the pillows Lili had bought the previous year. This wasn't duck down encased in Egyptian cotton.

I worked out that it wasn't just my head. The bed itself was on a tilt so my upper body was higher than my feet. The angle wasn't great, but it give me a view of the room. There wasn't much to see, but there was plenty to take in. I prayed my brain still knew how to process what my eyes saw. The first thing I registered was a black rectangle on the facing wall. It was a television, positioned conveniently in line with my head. It was turned on but I couldn't make out the programme. The volume had been muted, so there were no clues there. In any case, I was more interested in what I saw just below the set.

I used to think that all feet looked the same. But I knew the pair protruding from the end of the bed, those ten toes, were mine. No question. So why didn't they budge when I tried to move them?

In a strange way, this was even more disturbing than not being able to manipulate my own eyelids.

Who can't wiggle their own toes?

The body that the feet belonged to was dressed in the hospital gown I recalled from when I'd first been admitted. At least that hadn't changed. Underneath, I imagined, were my legs, my hips, my stomach.

I decided to pick a particular body part and focused on my knees. First my left, then my right. I concentrated hard, channelling the sort of intensity I used regularly on the free weights at the gym. I imagined my face contorting, straining as I would when trying to open a tight jar. I pictured my knee jerking upwards, violently kicking off the gown and leaving me naked on the bed.

Nothing happened. The gown continued to protect my modesty. My knee never twitched.

But then I noticed something else *was* moving.

Yes! There was definite movement further up my body, right at the lower limit of my vision as I looked directly ahead. My gown was rising with my chest. Of course, I was breathing. It had to go up, like it had to go down. Up, down, up, down.

Seeing that regular rise and fall of the gown distracted me for a minute or two. I wondered how many breaths a person might take in a lifetime. I tried to work it out. Average fifteen breaths a minute, I'd read somewhere during my police medical training. Multiply that by sixty for an hour, then by twenty-four, then by seven, then by fifty-two ...

My head was swimming. I was up to nearly eight million breaths a year, give or take. Times that by sixty ...

Almost half a billion. Yet I'd never thought about a single one of them. Before now.

At least that's working, I thought, as I remembered the nurse talking about my failing diaphragm in the trauma room. And as it was working, I reasoned, I should be able to control it. Kids hold their breath, swimmers hold their breath, townies visiting farmyards for the first time hold their breath. I'd been all three. I could do this.

Concentrate.

Nothing happened.

It might not be the most natural thing in the world to try to shut off your own breathing, but I was pretty sure I knew how to do it. I focused on locking my chest still, trapping the air in my lungs and holding it there. No inhaling, no exhaling.

But my chest continued to rise and fall, rise and fall, up and down. Almost as though it were not part of me at all.

I tried to work out what was happening. And while I did that I was conscious of the noises around me for the first time since waking up. One sounded like someone using bellows on a fire, just as I'd done during the winter months in Nebraska when I'd been Sheriff of Clay County. I knew there wouldn't be an open fire in a medical centre. If anywhere was guaranteed to have a generator producing its heat, it was the Queen of the Valley. But the whoosh of air being forced through a tube was unmistakable, as was the squeal of the bellows as they sucked, reset and gathered more air to blow.

Instinctively, I tried to turn my head. But my neck was as unresponsive as everything else.

It was then that I learned I couldn't even move my eyes in the direction of the noise.

My mind was already reeling with the growing list of bodily

functions I'd always taken for granted and now couldn't control. From breathing to blinking, I seemed to have lost power over all of them. But discovering that my eyes could only stare forwards was the biggest shock of all. The balls felt glued in their sockets. I couldn't make them pivot right or left.

What about up and down?

Same story. Zero movement. Not even a twitch. It was one thing not being able to open and close my eyelids on command, but not being able to glance even a millimetre to the left or right was utterly terrifying.

I'm going to be looking at that TV for ever.

I don't know how long I pondered that eventuality. Given my predicament, it might seem a minor issue, but it became all consuming. Left, right, up, down. Left, right, up, down. I pushed myself harder than I ever had at the gym to get some response, *any* response, but it was like trying to will a car engine to start without turning the key in the ignition. I didn't have the tools to do it. Worse than that, I didn't even know *how* to do it. Isolating the specific brain commands to make my eyeballs turn at that moment was as likely as my splitting the atom. Where would I even start?

It was a chastening moment. I'd been alive for sixty years and I'd never given a thought to how my body actually worked.

And now I was paying the price.

We've all heard doctors and scientists saying that the human brain is the world's most powerful computer. But how many of us have ever given that statement more than a moment's consideration? I know I never had before. But right then, lying in that bed, staring directly ahead, it was all I could think about.

I'm no computer expert, but I know they are logical. They respond to specific commands in predictable ways. They process information and get you from A to B. So, if my brain was a powerful computer, I figured I just needed to come up with the right commands.

I don't know how long I lay there trying to do just that. It seemed like hours but it could have been no more than a few seconds. It was impossible to keep track of time. I couldn't even work out how long I'd been unconscious. Had the doctor injected me half an hour earlier or a month ago? I had no way of knowing, but I honestly didn't care. Losing track of time is nothing compared with losing control of your own eyes.

Eventually, though, I was forced to admit defeat. The best neurologists in the world are only just starting to learn how to reboot the human brain, so what chance did I have?

Paradoxically, as soon as I resigned myself to staring forwards like a shop mannequin, the rest of the room drifted back into my consciousness. I might not have been able to see what was causing the wheezing noise, but I had been a police officer for twenty-five years and during that time I had developed other skills, honed other senses.

I noticed that there was a consistent rhythm to the sound. And that rhythm was in perfect step with something else – my breaths. My chest rose and fell at exactly the same rate as the machine sighed and wheezed. It was almost as though the two were connected.

But surely that was impossible? The noise was far away to my right. For my breathing to be related to whatever was causing it I'd have to be linked to it. And for that to be the case there would have to be some sort of . . .

Pipe.

It suddenly seemed so obvious. With my investigative background, not to mention my common sense, I should have been able to work it out much sooner. Then again, why would anyone ever think they were breathing through a machine on the other side of the room? It's just not something you expect when you wake up.

As I continued to dwell on how I could have missed something so obvious, I realised there was another reason why I hadn't been able to join up the dots. I wasn't losing my sharpness. My brain was working as well as ever, but it was working in a new way. It was keeping secrets from me. Not to thwart me, but to protect me.

As Jack Nicholson said in the movie *A Few Good Men*, 'You want the truth? You can't handle the truth.' And your brain knows that. It knows what you're capable of processing without freaking out, and it does its best to shroud you from anything that falls outside that category. I'd seen it hundreds of times on call-outs. People with the most horrific injuries can explain calmly and precisely what has happened to them as if they're suffering no more than a splinter. In order to hold you together in moments of crisis, the brain keeps you facing away from the truth for as long as possible. It cocoons you in a kind of blissful bubble of ignorance to stop you breaking down completely.

That's the logic. That's the neurological explanation.

And that, I surmised, was the only reason why I wasn't already insane.

'I had to leave when they started the intubation.'

Again, Lili is talking to someone outside my field of vision. It's clearly a friend this time. She sounds open and emotional. It's not her 'professional' voice, anyway.

'Suddenly it was action stations. Then I was ushered out of there. Nicely, of course. But they had jobs to do.'

'You know what it's like,' another voice says.

'Yes, I do. But it's hard!'

After a few seconds the other voice says, 'You know he's in the best place, don't you?'

'Of course. They've been amazing. When they transferred Rich from the Emergency Room they had to take him off the ventilator. So the nurse just walked alongside him, hand-pumping his breath. I've seen some things, Pat, but that was incredible.'

Pat? I know her. I recognise the name, and now the voice too. She works at the hospice. We've met a couple of times. It's good of her to come all the way across town to keep Lili company.

Or has she done nothing of the kind?

She takes care of the dying, as does Lili.

Maybe the 'best place' isn't the Queen of the Valley. Maybe they've transferred me to the hospice.

Maybe I'm about to die.

I knew I wasn't in a good way. I couldn't move a single muscle in my body. A machine was breathing for me. I was, to all intents and purposes, a slab of meat on a butcher's block connected to an electric socket. Was there any way back from here?

Obviously someone thought so. Why else would the doctors go to so much trouble to keep me alive? There has to be a point where even the most devoted medic says, 'Enough is enough' and turns off the machines. One of Lili's colleagues once told me that a lot of long-term cancer sufferers finally succumb to death only when their fluids and food are turned off. That decision is made by other humans, not by the patient. Similar humans seemed to have decreed that I was worth saving – but for how long? If I really was in the hospice, it was surely only a matter of time …

No! I refuse to accept it. There's too much going on in this room for it to be a hospice. They're not waiting for me to die. They're doing their best to save me.

At least that was what I had to hope.

Desperate for any sort of proof that I wasn't at the end of the medical line, I summoned all my energy to examine the rest of my surroundings. But trying to take in anything that wasn't directly in front of me without the ability to move my eyeballs was an enormous challenge. My focus was fixed in the mid-distance, on the television, the end of my bed and my feet. Anything else, anything closer to my head or off to the side, lost clarity depending on its distance from the far wall. Anyone who wears glasses knows what it's like to scan a room without their prescription lenses. You can make out shapes and colours, but there's a certain amount of guesswork.

To the right of my chest I could see my arm lying dormant. The image was blurry and unfocused, and the arm itself, like everything else, wasn't responding to my instructions. But I had to assume it was mine, even though part of me wished it wasn't.

Before I'd been put to sleep, the doctor had inserted a single IV drip via the back of my hand. Now there was a whole row of ports. I counted four, two filled and two awaiting tubes, like sockets on a multi-board. The doctors were obviously expecting to have to hook me up to plenty more drugs and fluids.

I realised if I concentrated on my hand I could feel the point of incision where the drip fed into it. And if I really focused I was sure I could feel whatever fluid was in the bag on the nearby rail as it pulsed into my bloodstream. It was a weird sensation. An alien one. In fact, it downright hurt.

And I'm going to be hooked up to four of these?

There was something else I could still feel – and taste. *Rubber.* I remembered it had been the first thing I'd sensed when I'd woken – whenever that had been. Then it had been trampled over by so many other thoughts, fears and emotions. But now it was back, right at the front of my mind, teasing me.

It was around this time that I first became aware of just how painful my jaw was feeling. There was a persistent ache, a bit like when you've been laughing too hard, only much worse. This was genuine pain.

Is something wrong with my head as well?

I tried to focus, calling on everything I had. What was it I used to tell my pupils in forensic science?

'Work the clues.'

And this time I can't let my brain keep the truth from me.

Of course, I couldn't move my jaw, so there was no way to ease the pain by flexing it. My tongue was dead as well – but only, I realised now, in the sense that it was immobile. Even though it was lying beached on the floor of my mouth, I was still aware of it. I could still feel it. And I could still feel *with* it.

Focusing all of my concentration on my tongue, I realised that the pipe entered my mouth on one side. I could feel it on my lips, to the side of my tongue, rasping against the roof of my mouth and wedged tight against the back of my throat. But in front of my tongue there was something else. Something bigger.

Something made of rubber.

I guessed it must have been playing a role in keeping me alive, but I couldn't work out how. There were no sounds coming from it, no vibrations. There were no obvious links between it and a machine. It wasn't doing anything, as far as I could tell, apart from sitting there, large and angular, pressing against my teeth, giving me lockjaw and what must look like the worst fake smile in history.

I kept thinking, trying to work it out.

It smelled like a block of rubber, it tasted like a block of rubber and it felt like a block of rubber, so it was fairly safe to assume it was a block of rubber. But why would a doctor stick a block of rubber in a patient's mouth?

I could have kicked myself – if my legs had worked – when I finally figured it out. It was there to keep my teeth apart. Without it, there would have been no way to feed the pipe that was keeping me alive down my throat.

Proud as I was to work it out, the realisation left me more depressed than ever. It was one thing to suffer a stroke, undergo a CAT scan and be plugged into various machines. But was I really so ill that I couldn't be trusted not to bite my own breathing apparatus in half? Or even chomp through my own tongue? Obviously the Queen of the Valley medical team thought so.

It was a new low. The point when I realised just how helpless I'd become.

I might not have been in a hospice, but my life, as I knew it, was surely over.

CHAPTER SEVEN

Drip. Drip. Drip.

Apart from the lack of mobility, there's nothing wrong with my vision. I've got no control over where I look or when my eyes open and close, but I can see what's in front of me perfectly clearly when they are open.

There's nothing wrong with my ears, either. And I can feel. And taste. And, yes, the room reeks of detergent. So that's all five senses present and correct.

That has to be a good sign, surely?

Or will they all start to shut down, one by one?

I wonder which will go first. And which will I miss the most? I'm not enjoying the taste of rubber, the all-pervading clinical smell is overpowering, and I could do without feeling pain in various parts of my body. That leaves just hearing and eyesight.

Right here, right now, if I had to choose, I'd keep my eyesight. I need to see the faces of the people around me. Words tell you only what people want them too. I learned that as a police officer. With faces you tend to get nearer the truth.

Not that it matters right now because no one is talking to me anyway.

'He's little more than a vegetable.'

How many times had I heard that said about badly injured patients? And how long would it be before someone said it about me?

Maybe they'd already said it. I still didn't know how long I'd been unconscious.

I made an effort to study the rest of the room for the first time. Head and eyes still locked forwards, I could make out a window to my left, past the bank of machines and leads trailing from my hand. I let the shapes and colours wash over me and tried to match them with similar images in my memory. The window had a blind, but it was open. I could see the blue of the sky and what I imagined was the top of a tree, so I was probably on the second or third floor. The sky was closer to navy than azure, so did that mean it was early evening? My best guess was that it was about twelve hours since I'd suffered the stroke. But that was still a guess.

In reality, I didn't even know if it was the same day. The dark-blue sky could have indicated the following dawn. Or evening a day or two later. Or a week. Or a month. How could I know? There wasn't even a clock within my field of vision. I stared at the TV but it offered no further clues.

I couldn't even be sure that I was still in the Queen of the Valley. I'd pretty much discounted the possibility that I'd been transferred to Lili's hospice, but I'd only seen The Queen's ambulance bay, trauma room and basement scanning room when I was admitted. Now I was in another, smaller room. It could have been in any medical facility in the world.

But logic suggested I hadn't moved anywhere except a few storeys up from the basement.

What I could say for sure was that I was in an intensive-care unit. And I had to view that as a positive sign. Once again, my hazy knowledge of anatomy filtered into my mind. I wasn't brain-dead, I knew that much. And, as the brain controls everything else, I convinced myself it was just a matter of time before things started to pick up again. It was nothing more than a waiting game.

As long as my mind continues to function, I'm going to be okay.

I resumed my extremely limited exploration of the room. Below the TV was a little dresser with a mirror that was pointing away from me. For some reason, this annoyed me intensely.

What's the point of having a mirror if I can't see my reflection in it? Who's meant to look into it if not me?

I pictured nurses coming in to adjust their make-up and doctors checking their ties. Then I realised it wasn't pointing away from me by accident. Someone had decided I shouldn't be able to see my own reflection. Not yet. Not in my condition.

Thinking about it, that was probably for the best. Even if I could have walked over there and tilted it towards me, I knew I didn't want to. It was hard enough seeing the four docks in my hand and my body lying stiff and prone before me. I couldn't face seeing my mouth held open by a rubber block as well. Or the tube disappearing down my throat. I'd witnessed a lot of horrible scenes in my time, helped a lot of people in the most unpleasant circumstances. But it was easier when it was happening to someone else.

I'd already figured out that my own brain was shielding me from the full horror of my predicament. Now it seemed that the hospital staff were doing exactly the same thing.

And I was grateful to them for that.

A doctor's talking to Lili while he assesses me. He's explaining something about the IV stand. Several bags are hanging from it. I guess some of them are spares, or refills. Maybe they hold different cocktails of medication. I try to listen as he explains what each of them contains. It doesn't mean much to me but Lili nods. She's dealt with this sort of stuff for years. He says that apart from saline and general vitamins, they're also pumping me full of morphine mixed with an anaesthetic drug called propofol.

Later – maybe hours, maybe minutes; time is a blur now – she explains all of this to Pat.

'They can regulate his medication via the IV,' Lili says. 'If they need to sedate him, they'll increase the dosage. If they want to rouse him, they'll decrease it.'

'Do they think he will wake up?' Pat asks.

'They don't know. All they can say is they'll know within forty-eight hours if the clot buster has worked.'

'I'm sure he'll be okay.'

'He's got to be, Pat. He just has to be.'

I should be worried listening to this, but I'm not. Because I know something Lili and the doctors don't.

I'm already *awake.*

How long had my eyes been open? It felt like a couple of hours but it was probably just a few minutes, because I was still taking in the sights that lay directly ahead of me.

On the right-hand side of my field of vision, opposite the window, I could make out the blurry shape of a door. I struggled to bring it into focus but again my eye muscles wouldn't budge. If the door had been open I might have caught a glimpse of what was on the other side, which in turn might have helped me figure out where I was. I pictured myself walking through it. When would that be? Tomorrow? Next week? A month, maybe? I had no idea. I didn't have a clue how long strokes usually lasted. I just knew that I'd had one.

I knew something else, too. I needed to pee.

The familiar sensation came out of nowhere. One minute all of my attention was focused on trying to identify my surroundings. The next I couldn't think of anything other than emptying my bladder.

When had I last drunk anything? I racked my brain. Not since my regular cup of coffee this morning – assuming it was still the same day.

No, wait a minute.

I hadn't drunk anything before my shower. Lili had offered me a cup when she was having her breakfast but I'd said no. That should have told both of us something was up. When was the last time I'd turned down a cup of Joe?

So why did I need to pee? Surely you only have to get rid of what you put in, and I hadn't put a drop of liquid in my body for at least twelve hours. Did that mean, on top of everything else, I had some sort of prostate complication as well?

As I tried to work it out my attention returned to my hand and, more specifically, to one of the tubes that were sticking out of the back of it.

Of course, the drip.

I might not have had a drink, but liquid had still been entering my body ever since I'd arrived at the hospital. And, as I'd already realised, what goes in has to come out.

But how the hell am I going to pee? I can't get anywhere near a bathroom.

The urge continued to build inside me. I tried to fight it but I had nothing. I was an open door. As with every other part of my body, I could feel my bladder but I had no control over it. I willed someone to walk through the door and wheel me to a restroom. We could still make it if they hurried. But no one came.

Oh no, this is going to get messy.

My time was up. I felt the warm stream of urine as it passed through my penis and waited for the inevitable damp patch to spread across my gown and the bedsheets. My groin was just at the bottom of my field of vision, so there was no way to avoid the embarrassing sight.

But I waited, and waited, and nothing happened. The flow of urine stopped – I could sense that clearly. A few seconds passed, then a few minutes, but there was still no trace of damp. My thighs, as far as I could tell, were dry. The sheets beneath my legs and backside were, too. The gown was the same colour it had always been.

I started to doubt that I'd peed at all.

I weighed up the evidence. I was sure I hadn't imagined it. I knew what it felt like to pee. I'd relieved myself several times a day, every day of my life, and this had felt exactly the same.

Or had it? Now that no more liquid was flowing out of my body I realised that something else was coming out of my penis. And it hurt. Why hadn't I noticed it before? Because I hadn't needed to pee before, I supposed. Or because I was so caught up in trying to fathom what was going on in other parts of my body. Whatever the reason, I focused on it now.

There was still no stain on the gown. It was as though the pee had just vanished into thin air, or had been transported somewhere else as soon as it had left my body. How was that possible?

Suddenly it came to me.

Catheter.

I'd been fitted with a catheter. It was the only explanation. The doctors must have done it after they'd inserted the tube into my throat.

The thought of a tube running through my penis made me

feel sick. My instinct was to get it the hell out of there. I knew I couldn't move my arms but that didn't stop me trying. Every second that passed, I could feel the plastic more distinctly, cutting and burning and violating me in a way that no man should ever suffer.

Or so it seemed at the time. In reality, the 'pain' was little more than a slight tingle. It was more the thought of the catheter that sickened me. But when your thoughts are all you have, they're more important than you can imagine.

A second later, though, I realised I had a much bigger problem to worry about. My mouth was filling up again. Spittle was collecting in my throat. There wasn't too much of it yet, but that was still more than enough to send me into a panic. I was convinced I'd soon be drowning in my own saliva again.

What were they doing when I was under? I thought they were going to fix this! What the hell is the pipe for if liquid can still collect in my mouth?

Everything else paled into insignificance now. All of the other issues – the lack of control over my eyes, my useless limbs, the catheter – were bearable. But the sensation of drowning I'd felt as I'd been put under had been truly terrifying. I couldn't cope with it, couldn't think my way through it. And now it was happening again.

How long have I got?

Seconds? Minutes? Hours? I had no idea. But I knew the build-up of liquid could kill me unless I got help.

I would have dwelled on it longer but a sound from the corner of the room diverted my attention. Maybe this was the help I needed. At the periphery of my vision I saw the door open and a familiar figure walk in. I didn't need 20/20 eyesight to recognise my own wife. Three thoughts flashed through my mind.

I knew she wouldn't leave me here.

If there had been dry ice and a Hollywood orchestra playing she could not have made a better entrance.

I can't wait to see the look on her face when she sees I'm okay!

I knew I couldn't talk, but I also knew I'd been unconscious for some time. So Lili would be excited to see me awake. That alone would tell her I was recovering, on the mend. It might even ease the worry she was sure to be feeling.

A couple of strides brought her directly in front of the dresser. I could have cried as she looked me in the eyes.

'I'm awake!' I tried to shout. 'I'm okay!'

I knew nothing would come out of my mouth, but my eyes, my face, my whole soul were hollering the same message.

She stared at me for a few seconds, then turned round to face someone who was standing behind her.

'Still no change,' Lili said.

I recognised the second person as Pat, Lili's colleague from the hospice. They stood at the end of my bed, looked at me, then turned back to each other.

'I'm so sorry, Lili,' Pat said.

'So am I, Pat.'

'But Rich is a fighter. He's strong. They'll pull him through this.'

'I hope so, Pat, I really do.'

She didn't sound very sure. If anything, she looked close to tears. I couldn't understand why she was so upset. I was wide awake, listening to every word and studying every expression on her face. Couldn't she see that? Couldn't Pat? They were both healthcare professionals. Surely they knew when someone was trying to communicate with them, didn't they?

Or am I really that far gone?

I watched them continue their conversation. I still heard every word but now I couldn't take much in. The longer they stood there, the longer they chatted, the more depressed I became. It wasn't only that my own wife couldn't hear me. She wasn't even aware I was awake.

That realisation snapped me back to my major concern before the door had opened. Who was going to stop me drowning? I tried to banish the fear from my mind and tune back in to what Lili was saying. I needed information. I needed to know when I was going to get better. When was the clot buster going to kick in? And why wasn't this pipe in my mouth doing its job properly?

However, nothing Lili or Pat said shed any light on any of these questions. I was alone. It was up to me to work it all out.

And, about two seconds later, I pretty much did. Well, I figured out what was happening with the tube, anyway. The doctor had noticed I was struggling to breathe, so he'd hooked me up to the mechanical diaphragm that was still wheezing away on the other side of the room. Its job was to do my breathing for me, and I could feel it doing that perfectly well. But it had never been designed to vacuum up the spittle in my throat. The fact that I couldn't swallow was unrelated to the diaphragm issue.

Did the medics even know about this?

Drip. Drip. Drip.

I could picture the pool in my throat growing, a millilitre at a time.

Drip. Drip. Drip.

I tried again and again to communicate with Lili, willed her to get help, but she saw nothing, heard nothing. In desperation, I focused on Pat instead. Same result. Even though they were both looking directly at me, it was as though I wasn't really there.

Are they really just going to stand there and watch me drown?

I lost track of how long Lili and Pat remained at the foot of my bed. But after a while Pat turned to Lili and said she had to return to her shift.

'I'll pop back on my next break,' she promised.

'I don't know what I would have done without you,' Lili said. I could hear she meant every word.

I watched as an increasingly blurry Pat left the room, but then, as my thoughts turned back to Lili, I noticed the door hadn't fully closed. Someone was pushing it open again.

My heart leapt when they walked through and I realised it wasn't just Pat, coming to collect something she'd forgotten.

A nurse! Finally I'm going to get some help. Finally someone is going to tell me what the hell is going on with my body.

She greeted Lili warmly. They had obviously met before. Perhaps that was a clue to how long I'd been lying in that bed.

'Any change?' the nurse asked.

'Not yet,' Lili said.

If only you knew . . .

I was pretty sure I hadn't seen the nurse before. Although, as she bustled around to my right, I recognised the badge on her uniform. Just as I'd thought, I was in the ICU – the Queen of the Valley's intensive-care unit. So, they hadn't felt the need to transfer me to another hospital. But there was no doubt that I was in a very bad way. Critical, in fact.

'I'm so sorry it took so long to get him in here,' the nurse said. 'We just don't have the beds.'

'It's not your fault,' Lili replied.

'I know, but it's not right that a man in Rich's position should have to wait three hours.'

Lili nodded. She understood.

And, for the first time since waking up, so did I. Finally I had some information. Not only was I still at The Queen; it sounded like it was just a few hours since I'd suffered the stroke. I'd had to wait in line for an available room in the ICU, but now, at some point in the afternoon, that's where I was. Delays like this were getting more and more common, according to Lili and her medical friends. Most hospitals simply didn't have the resources to cope with the huge demand. I'd heard of patients being left on trolleys in corridors, passageways and waiting rooms. Lili never would have allowed me to be treated like that. But I couldn't help wondering where I'd been for the past three hours.

The nurse looked me over from head to foot, then examined the tubes coming out of my hand. Then she walked out of my field of vision, presumably to check on the ventilator. Seemingly satisfied, she came back into view, reached over to a cart and grabbed another bag of what looked like saline. In a rapid motion she plugged it into one of the empty ports on the back of my hand. The whole exercise took no more than ten seconds. Maybe she knew that Lili was in the same profession and was keen to display her skills. Either way, everything was done absolutely textbook.

Her tasks complete, she turned as though to leave the room.

'What about my spit?' I tried to call out.

The nurse stopped dead in her tracks.

Did she hear me?

She turned back and went to fetch something else away to my right. Then she returned, stood over my face, like a dentist, and peered inside my mouth.

'Ahh, you've got a little bit of spittle building up there, Rich,' she said. 'Let's get rid of that for you.'

I wasn't sure what made me happier – hearing she was going to stop me drowning or just the fact that she spoke to me as though I could understand everything she said. Which I could, despite what everyone else was thinking.

She produced a small pipe about the size of a pencil with a curly cable trailing behind it and pushed it towards my mouth. I knew instantly from the noise that it was a suction pump, like the ones used to suck up liquids and bits of tooth or filling during dental work.

Yes!

I didn't care that she had to knock against the pipe going down my throat in order to get at the pool of saliva beneath my tongue. I didn't care that it felt like fingernails scraping down my larynx. I didn't care about anything at that moment, aside from the fact that this wonderful woman was saving my life. It seemed I wasn't going to die that day after all.

Unfortunately, though, some people thought I already had.

CHAPTER EIGHT

It's Okay to Go

Someone else is entering the room. Lili and the nurse both turn towards the door. The new arrival is wearing a long white coat which marks him out as a doctor. He's not one of the guys I saw downstairs. He picks up my notes from where they're hanging at the foot of the bed and makes a few comments to the nurse. She reaches over to the IV stand again, but I can't see what she does there.

In fact, within minutes, I can't see anything at all. Whatever she did, it's shutting me down. I try to resist but the urge to sleep is too strong.

Was it possible my eyes were already open *before* I woke up? I knew sharks slept like that, but could humans? Perhaps with the drugs that were flooding through my body, I could.

I noticed that the programme on the TV had changed. Time had moved on while I'd been asleep. Then I noticed it was darker outside the window. Was it nighttime? Or the following morning? If she'd been there, I would have checked what Lili was wearing. If she were dressed differently, I'd know for sure that a day had passed. But she wasn't there. Nobody was.

Where was Lili? Had she gone home without saying goodbye?

Had she gone to the canteen for some food? The anxiety of wondering where she was had almost overpowered me in the ambulance. Now, though, I was okay. I knew she had to have her reasons for leaving me. I was positively chilled about it. In fact, I was chilled about everything.

What had changed? Apart from the nurse connecting me to a new IV bag, I couldn't recall anything out of the ordinary. Was it possible some new drugs were filtering into my body and altering my mood? From the little I knew of morphine, it was a painkiller. From the even less I knew of propofol, it was an anaesthetic. Obviously they were keeping the pain in my body in check. But could they be affecting my mind as well? I had no way of knowing for sure.

But, for whatever reason, I wasn't scared. Not by the block of rubber between my teeth, not by the tubes invading my penis and my throat, not even by the fact that I couldn't blink. Since waking up for the first time in this room I'd gone from claustrophobia via depression, terror, panic and misery to a sort of peace. Why? Nothing had got better. I hadn't made a miraculous full recovery. I hadn't even made a partial one. Yet one minute I was convinced I was going to die, and the next I wasn't. For some reason, the predicament in which I found myself just didn't seem to matter. I became resigned to the fact that there was nothing I could do about it.

Actually, that wasn't entirely true. There was one thing I could do. I could survive. I could give my body the time to repair itself and I could eventually get out of that bed and onto my feet.

No more thoughts of death, I decided. I had to be positive.

Something's on my calf. I can feel it. A fly or a bug, maybe? Perhaps a small spider has crawled under my gown? I can feel every step. For a moment, it's all I can sense. Like when I knew I had to pee, it completely overrides all my other senses. Every available part of my brain is directed towards the tiny pitter-patter up and down my leg, and the sensation of tiny hairs springing back into shape. If I concentrate hard, I reckon I'll even be able to count the number of legs stepping on me. Six or eight? Fly or spider? I'll know soon enough.

But I can't count the footsteps. All I can tell for sure is they're light as a feather – and just as ticklish.

No, no, no. Stop moving. Whatever you are, buzz off.

It feels like a feather being dragged across my skin.

Get the hell off, fly!

I try to exhale, to blow it away. Nothing. I try to twitch my leg to shake it off. Same result.

Having an itch and not being able to scratch it is the worst feeling in the world. Anyone who's ever worn a plaster cast on their arm or leg will acknowledge that. It drives you crazy. You want to break off that plaster and get inside, even if it means your bones will never heal.

I don't have any broken bones but I do have useless limbs.

Lili is back at the foot of the bed now. Same clothes – must be the same day. Or did she stay overnight? It doesn't matter right now. I will her – beg her – to swat the fly away. She doesn't move.

This is almost as terrifying as the spittle build-up in my mouth.

Has Lili even noticed? Why would she? Why would she know that I'm being tickled to death and there's nothing I can do about it?

I must have fallen asleep again, because I woke to find at least one medic buzzing around my wires, tubes and machines. Lili didn't budge, except to let them pass. The doctors examined my charts and compared them to readings they took on the machines. Then they had conversations with the nurse in hushed tones. What didn't they want me to hear?

But then I realised it wasn't my feelings they were trying to protect. It was Lili's.

They still don't know I can hear them.

Earlier, I would have panicked. This time I didn't. Maybe it was the drugs, or maybe I was just determined to stay calm. I thought of playing my guitar, of gardening, of riding the Harley, of reading late at night, of cruising in my patrol car and of pumping iron at the gym. I loved to do all of these things. And I did them all on my own, always had done. I could easily go half a day without speaking to another living soul. Longer sometimes, especially when clocking up the miles in my Ford Crown Victoria back in Nebraska.

So not speaking to anyone now wasn't such a big deal. I just wished Lili looked happier.

When you are in the eye of the storm you simply live through it the best you can. That's what I was doing. But poor Lili was on the outside, helpless and having to respond to something she didn't understand. In that respect, I figured I was more comfortable with my predicament than she was. I wished there was something I could do to reassure her.

Eventually, she moved round to the side of the bed. From the scraping sound on the floor, I guessed she had a chair there. She was physically closer to me now, but she seemed further away. I could hear her breathing and smell her perfume, but she'd become no more than a cloud on the extremity of my peripheral vision. I desperately wanted to see her more clearly, but trying to focus hurt my eyes, so in the end I gave up and let my mind relax. Just knowing she was there was still a comfort. I could settle for that.

Who am I kidding?

Having my wife so close but not being able to hold her and

tell her everything was going to be all right was torture. More than anything in the world, I wanted to wrap my arms around her and never let her go.

I think she must have read my mind.

I felt her pick up my hand, and the touch sent an electric shock through my body. Suddenly all my physical receptors were concentrated in that hand. I could make out every millimetre of her palm and fingers as they wrapped around mine. When she squeezed tight I was convinced that I would make it through this.

The nurse is humming a tune as she walks through the door. Occasionally she adds a few lyrics, but I don't recognise them. They're English, that's as much as I can tell.

She walks over and I sense her stop at my machines. I hear the scratching of pen on paper as she fills in her clipboard files. Then she runs her hand over my brow.

I hear her tut.

Then she swats away the fly and shoos it out of the window.

I love you, nurse. Thank you so much.

I was getting used to waking up.

Each time initially felt like the start of a new day. I would go through the process of wondering where I was, suddenly remember, then relive the trauma of what had happened to me. All in a split second. All before my breathing machine had pumped out a single breath. Then I would work out that only an hour or so had elapsed since I'd fallen asleep. I could tell that much from the deepening colour of the sky outside the window and the people in the room.

My eyes were always already open whenever I woke up. I wondered if I did that subconsciously, in the instant before waking.

The only way to find out was to try to close them again. I ignored the block between my teeth, the drips in my hand and the pipe in my throat and channelled everything I had into lowering my eyelids. They didn't budge. I kept trying, counting the mechanical breaths. After ten I gave up.

At least they're open and not shut.

It was a small mercy, but one worth clinging to.

Next on my checklist was my left hand. I'd remembered Lili holding it. Just that recollection made me smile inside. I couldn't feel her now, though. At the edge of my vision, I saw that my hand was indeed empty. Perhaps it hurt her back or her arm to stretch across like that for any length of time.

I tried to make out the cloudy blur past my left shoulder. It seemed to have disappeared. I listened for Lili's breath, or the sound of her chair scraping on the floor. Instinctively, I tried to hold my own breath in order to hear better. Then I realised how ridiculous I was being. I could think about holding my breath all I liked, but the ventilator was going to keep pumping me full of air whether I liked it or not. How could I forget something so noisy?

In the end, I had to accept that Lili wasn't there. But not for long. At that moment, the door opened and she walked back into the room. Only this time she wasn't alone.

Shannon!

I watched as my daughter came running towards the foot of my bed. Then I watched her stop dead in her tracks as she saw me. She was followed by my grandchildren, Reina and Jacob, and their father Roger. He nodded to Shannon, put his arms around the kids and backed them out of the door even before they'd got fully inside. Then Shannon broke down into a flood of tears.

It's one thing seeing your wife going through hell. It's another witnessing your own flesh and blood so distraught, especially when you're the reason. I'd caused my daughter to cry. Happy as I was that she'd come, I couldn't bear to see her like this. Yet I couldn't look away. I couldn't even close my eyes.

Why doesn't Roger get her out of here, too?

Shannon's hands were covering her face, as if she were trying to blow her nose. But we all knew she wasn't. Lili went straight over and tried to comfort her.

Shannon is my middle child, born in 1971. Either side of her are Michelle, two years her senior, and Melanie, three years her junior, all born to my first wife, Sandra. After being dragged by me and my work from the west coast to the east coast, then into the middle, it was no surprise that they'd all ended up scattered around the country. That meant our meetings were not as frequent as I would have liked, but it had the added consequence that none of them knew Lili at all. In the couple of years we'd been married, we'd all met up just once. I wondered how Lili had even got hold of Shannon. I guessed she must have gone through my cellphone's address book. Was that what she'd been doing when I'd woken up to find her gone? Making the hardest phone call of her life?

Now I had something else to feel guilty about.

Lili led Shannon round the side of the bed and to the chair just by my shoulder. In the corner of my eye I saw her sit down, still sobbing. Lili was standing next to her, more to the centre of my vision. She was fighting back tears of her own. What was going through her head? Did she want Shannon to be strong in front of me? Or was she wishing she could let go herself? I guessed Lili's training had taught her to temper all emotion. But she had to be hurting inside. I didn't need to see it on her face to know that.

I wished with all my heart that I could at least move my eyes to look directly at my wife and daughter, to show them I was aware they were there. They must have known they were in my heart. I just wanted them to know I knew they were in the room.

'Oh, Dad,' Shannon said through her hands, 'I'm so sorry.'

I wanted to reach out and comfort her. I wanted to leap up and say, 'Look, it's just a stroke. People recover from them all the time. I'll be up and walking in no time.'

Instead, I lay there, staring at the mute TV, listening to my daughter sob.

'Did you manage to get hold of your sisters?'

Lili is talking to Shannon. They're both standing by the window now. I don't remember them moving over there. Have I been asleep again?

'Michelle will be here as soon as she can.'

Michelle's coming here? All the way from Alabama? I wish I could tell her not to bother. I don't want her to see me like this. Why doesn't she just wait till I'm better? I won't be offended. I know she loves me.

Then I remember there's no point telling my eldest daughter to do anything, even when I'm able to . . .

'I think she's bringing one of her girls,' Shannon continues. 'Although I'm beginning to regret bringing my kids. It's not how I want them to remember their grandpa. I'm glad Roger's here, though.'

'It's lucky you live so close,' Lili says.

Vacaville, Shannon's home, is only about forty miles away, which is why she was able to get here so quickly. Michelle will have to fly. As will Melanie, if she's decided to come too.

It's like Shannon has read my mind.

'I think Melanie's probably at St Louis airport right now,' she says. 'She's coming to mine when she arrives and I'll drive her in tomorrow.'

I really wish they wouldn't go to so much trouble. Although, I have to admit, it will be nice to see them all together.

A sense of contentment washes over me as I drift off to sleep again.

Shannon's reaction when she came through the door told me everything I needed to know about how bad I looked. It confirmed that the hospital staff had been right to keep the dresser mirror pointing away from me. But once she had calmed down she went back outside and returned with my grandchildren.

Many people would say that kids should not be exposed to the goings-on inside hospitals, but I don't agree with that. I was glad to see them. And, to their credit, they handled the sight of me a lot better than their mother had done.

I'm sure they've seen much worse in a computer game.

Roger stood silently behind them. In fact, everyone remained quiet. Even though there were now eight people in the room, including a doctor, a nurse and me, it was quieter than it had ever been.

And I didn't like it.

The lack of conversation meant I could hear every clank and whirr of my breathing apparatus. I could hear every beep from the machine measuring my heart rate. And, I realised with alarm, I could hear the gurgle of spittle in my own throat.

Oh, sweet lord. It's starting again.

But no sooner had that thought entered my mind than the door opened and one of the doctors from earlier returned. He didn't check any of the machines this time. Instead, he made a bee-line straight for me, took a quick look in my mouth and started readying the suction pump. Two minutes later he was sucking the liquid from my throat, and he didn't stop until he had siphoned up every last drop of moisture.

As horrific as it sounds, having my mouth vacuumed was one of the highlights of my day. But it proved too much for Shannon. As the doctor left I realised it was just Lili and me in the room now. The old team, together again. Us against the world.

With Lili at my side, I honestly felt I could take on all-comers. We were invincible.

Which was why I was so surprised by what happened a short while later, after Shannon and her family had left for the evening. The darkness beyond the window told me it was definitely well into the night now. I had no idea exactly how much time had passed, but I did know that Lili had been at my side for most of the day, and I guessed she needed to go home too, if only to get some sleep and freshen up. I wasn't looking forward to her saying goodbye, though.

Nor was she, by the look of it. She seemed nervous.

She leaned over, kissed me on the cheek and hugged me tight. That much I liked. I only wished I could have responded in a similar way.

But then she pulled back, squeezed my hand again and, staring deep into my unblinking eyes, said, 'It's okay to go, honey. Don't worry about me. I'll be all right.'

I could see in her face that she didn't expect to see me again.

After one more kiss she turned and left the room.

CHAPTER NINE

The Conversation

I like the National Geographic channel. Programmes about animals, wildlife and the planet's natural resources all appeal to me. Reality shows with human beings I can take or leave. But fly-on-the-wall stuff with leopards, meerkats and mini-beasts are right up my street.

The sound on the TV is now set just high enough for me to hear. When the nurse comes in to check on my dials and tubes she can't help looking up and admiring the pride of big cats hunting their prey in the African bush. Even as she checks my mouth for saliva I can tell she's listening to the narration.

I know I am.

While my latest puddle of spittle is being suctioned I try to see past the hand and keep track of what's on the screen. Partly to take my mind off what's going on in my mouth, partly because I'm genuinely interested. Animals are so pure. Strong beats weak, fast beats slow, big beats small. It really is survival of the fittest out there.

But I can't see the TV, so my mind eventually wanders back to my condition. Twenty-four hours ago I thought I was one of the fittest. I was certainly among that number at my gym. Maybe I couldn't compete with guys half my age, but anyone forty-plus would have trouble pinning me down. Am

I a leader of the pack? Probably not. That's not my style. But the rest know not to mess with me.

Or at least they used to.

I try to imagine the animals on the TV show experiencing what I'm going through. It's not a happy thought, and it definitely doesn't have a happy ending. I know they'd be torn to pieces, if not by their own kind then by the predators hanging around the periphery of the herd. Then anything that was left would be picked clean by the vultures circling overhead.

But I'm not an animal. I'm not fodder for the predators. I'm alive. I might not be well at the moment, but I'm a fighter. I'm not fighting to the death. I'm fighting death itself. So why did Lili say goodbye? It's not my time yet. I just know it.

The nurse finishes siphoning my spittle and I get a clear view of the TV once more. Although not for long. She adjusts something on my IV stand and then flicks off the programme via the remote control.

'Time to sleep,' she says, and leaves the room.

Seconds later, I do as I'm told.

My life was a series of people entering and leaving the room. People would rush in, people would rush out. It was like watching a play. A farce. Except no one knew the joke. No one except me.

They all think I'm dying – but I know I'm not.

I couldn't wait to see the looks on their faces when they realised they'd been had.

The mini-vacuum cleaner was clearing my throat again. A different person was operating it this time but the skill level was the same. I heard the tube clunking against the pipe and the rubber block but there was little discomfort. By now I was getting used to the sensation of so much apparatus in my mouth. I promised myself that I would never take breathing and swallowing for granted again. And it was just a matter of time before I would get to keep that promise. I was confident of that.

Nurses and doctors came and went. Machines, dials and clipboards were consulted, adjusted and amended. The TV was switched on again. A programme about the Arctic filled the screen. I pictured myself living there. Miles from anywhere, self-sufficient, strong and happy.

Maybe one day I might persuade Lili to travel up there with me?

No chance. The second we had any money, I knew we would be heading straight to her beloved Hawaii.

I was awake when she returned to the room, but I couldn't tell if she was surprised to find me alive and waiting for her. She certainly looked tired, but she was as beautiful as ever, especially when she smiled.

She sat with me through two TV programmes – around an hour, I guessed – during which time a series of medics came in and chatted to each other in hushed, professional tones as they weighed up my progress. While I willed them to talk *to me*, I began to feel a familiar rumbling in my stomach. Actually, it was a little below my stomach.

I realised it was time to take another leak, so I prepared myself for the involuntary flood. I'd got beyond the embarrassment by then. I just wanted the relief to come as quickly as possible. But even as I felt the catheter starting to fill with liquid, I knew there was something else going on. Something bigger.

The second I realised what my body was up to, I started racking my brain for some memory of a catheter for back passages. Surely there had to be one. How else did bedridden patients defecate? They couldn't just go in their beds.

Could they?

I knew that my face wasn't betraying any discomfort or panic.

But I could feel the movement in my bowels as things started to happen. Scary, familiar things. But even if I could have stopped myself, what would be the point? It would only have to come out later. Mortified by that realisation, I tried to focus on Lili sitting quietly next to me.

What now?

I struggled to halt my bowels' progress, but to no effect. Finally, at the point of no return, I had no option but to allow nature to take its course. Lili was talking to one of the doctors at the time. Neither of them was even looking in my direction. It was only when a nurse walked in a few minutes later and announced, 'I think Rich needs changing' that they twigged.

I can honestly say I had never been so embarrassed.

In my life, I'd been shot at, attacked, threatened and injured in various ways. Yet none of that compared to the agony I suffered over the next few minutes.

The nurse hurried out of the room and returned with a male colleague carrying a bowl and what looked like a towel. She lifted up the sheet covering my body and pulled at my gown as her colleague rolled my lower half over. I couldn't really see what they were doing, and I didn't want to watch anyway, but it was mesmerising, especially when I spotted some sort of muslin wrap under my gown.

I'm wearing a diaper! When on earth did they put that on me?

I supposed it was around the time I was hooked up to the machinery in the room. But I was surprised I hadn't felt it. Maybe it was another truth my brain felt I wasn't ready to handle. There are some things that men are just not programmed to do – or have done to them. Having two nurses change your diaper and clean your backside is certainly one of them. I couldn't think of anything more humiliating.

The one slight relief was that I guessed Lili had seen it all before. But that was on other people, other men, strangers. No wife should witness such a thing happening to her own husband. How could a marriage survive after an episode like that?

Then I remembered. She had already given me her blessing to die. She wasn't thinking about our long-term future, about our marriage, about us. She was just trying to send me off in as comfortable a fashion as possible.

Even during the ignominy of the bed bath, I found my mind dwelling on what she'd said the previous evening. Why had she said goodbye? I was in a bad way but I was getting better, I knew that. Or if I wasn't yet, I soon would be. What had given her the idea that my time was up? Was she just being sentimental or had Shannon said something to trigger it all? Maybe just her reaction to seeing me had pushed Lili over the edge? I wished I could have shown them both that I was still in the room. Lili was so used to nursing patients through to the end of their lives that I decided she'd slipped prematurely into hospice mode with me.

Just you wait. I'll surprise you yet.

For all my bravado, though, it kept eating away at me. She'd said goodbye. She'd given me her blessing to pass away. I was confident that wasn't going to happen, but what if I was wrong? Would she recover? Would she remarry? Would she even remember me in a few years' time?

Life for me without Lili was unthinkable. But so was the idea of her living without me. I'm not proud of it, but the thought was definitely there. Of course, I only wanted her to be happy, but deep inside was the tiny spark of jealousy that someone else might take my place by her side further down the line.

Put it out of your mind. That's not going to happen.

But part of me still believed that it was.

I suppose it took around ten minutes for the nurses to clean me up and fit a fresh diaper. They did it just in time. As they left, the door opened and Shannon walked in. I couldn't imagine how she would have handled seeing her daddy having his ass wiped.

I was pleased to see her again, but even happier to see the person behind. Melanie, still my baby girl, even though she was now thirty-five. It was a six-hour flight from St Louis, so she couldn't have had much sleep. Behind her came one of her sons. He smiled at me, which I'll never forget. After that, though, his eyes stayed rooted to the floor. I didn't mind. It must have been hard for him. But I didn't know whether he was afraid of embarrassing himself or me.

As much as I love all my daughters, Melanie's visit was a tonic that the Queen of the Valley just couldn't give me, a real shot in the arm. We couldn't shut her up as a child and we couldn't shut her up now. Thank goodness. The previous afternoon had felt like a wake. Lili, Shannon and her family, the staff and Pat had all come and gone in virtual silence. That wasn't Melanie's style. She was the glue that held all three sisters together and it was exactly the same in that ICU room. She got Lili and Shannon talking and, whenever they dried up, she filled in the gaps. It was so refreshing to hear them chatting away to each other, even though they'd been brought together by something so terrible. All we needed now was Michelle to make the party complete.

I could have listened to my girls talking all day. Maybe I did. I was still unable to gauge the passage of time. The next thing I noticed was my drip being tweaked yet again. I knew the drill by now, knew what awaited me in a few seconds' time.

Please be here when I wake up.

My wish came true. Even before my vision returned, I could hear the familiar voices I'd left behind. Only this time there was an additional one. No, more than one. I recognised Michelle's voice instantly. I was so glad to hear her that I could have cried. It took me a few more seconds to place the other one, and I needed my sight to help me out. But even as my vision came back into focus, I couldn't believe who I was looking at.

Steve.

Steve Logan, my old school buddy. I'd played in the woods with him, listened to records with him, first joined a gym with him. We had so much shared history and even after he'd moved up to Washington State we'd stayed in touch. And now he was here.

Oh, well played, Lili.

Calling my daughters was one thing. But tracking down Steve was incredible. I was so glad she'd managed to do it.

Yet I was confused, too. Why was he here? It wasn't as though I was at death's door.

'You've got quite a crowd out there,' one of the nurses says.

Melanie laughs. 'The more the merrier. Dad's a popular guy.'

'There must be thirty-five people,' Shannon adds, returning to the room. 'I don't know where half of them are going to sit.'

'Why don't we go out and give some of the others a chance?' Melanie suggests.

Lili nods, apparently glad to leave the decision-making to someone else.

I don't know how long Steve stayed. Time seemed to drag. He didn't have much to say. Not to me, anyway. Melanie got more out of him. When she didn't ask a direct question, however, he clammed up. Eventually he got up to leave. He thanked Lili for inviting him, then looked me straight in the eye.

'Goodbye, old friend,' he said.

'Goodbye, buddy,' I wanted to call back. 'I'll get up to Seattle soon, I promise. It's definitely my turn to visit now.'

But he was gone before I'd even finished thinking it.

No sooner had he left than another visitor arrived. This one surprised me even more than Steve. It was Elsa, my third wife. What an amazing thing for Lili to do. What other woman would think of inviting her husband's ex at a time like that?

Elsa and I had remained on good terms after the divorce, to such an extent that there weren't many people I would rather have seen waltzing through the door. My face may not have shown it, but I really wanted to smile. And I felt the same sensation time and again over the next few hours.

Lili had clearly been very busy with my contacts book. After my daughters, my best friend and my ex-wife, a whole line of people, friends and family, made their way to my bedside. In truth, it was all a bit overwhelming. Some of them were joint friends of Lili and me, couples we saw on a regular basis, like Keith and Pam Reuter and David and Colleen Topper. Others I hadn't seen for years. There were guys from the force, more old friends from school, even my younger sister, Carol, drove up. And they were just the ones I saw. Slipping in and out of consciousness, or sleep, or whatever the doctors called it, I was aware that some people must have been and gone without me ever noticing them. After all, nobody seemed to be able to tell whether I was awake or not. But those I did see made me feel like a million dollars.

It was great to see one guy in particular. My second wife, Linda, had been a nurse as well, and one day she'd introduced me to one of her patients, a young guy called Eric who'd been in a motorcycle accident. I think she'd thought it would be good for him to talk to a fellow bike nut. He was twenty-five years younger than me but we instantly hit it off. He was as brave and strong as you can get – he had to be, because he was paralysed from the neck down as a result of the accident. He didn't let quadriplegia and living in a wheelchair destroy his life, but even so, it was obviously hard for him. So seeing his smiling face across the room from me that afternoon was really something special. I couldn't begin to think what kind of a journey he'd had to undertake to reach me.

Eric was one of the chattier ones. Maybe because he knew what it was like to be lying in the hospital bed. Most people, though, were like Shannon and Steve: tongue-tied, sad and seemingly at their wits' end. They all wanted to appear upbeat but most of them struggled to keep any momentum in the conversation once they realised they would get no reaction from me. I think it was usually a blessing when they were ushered out by a nurse after their five or so minutes were up.

A lot of people entertain the idea of attending their own funeral to see what kind of a turnout they get. I realised soon after Eric had left that I was experiencing my own send-off right there and then. And, I have to say, I was pretty pleased with the number of people who took the time to come. Pleased and honoured. It was a conveyor belt of all the people who meant the most to me. They'd all come to pay their respects and say their farewells.

But I didn't want their farewells or their tears. And I certainly didn't want to see my nearest and dearest looking so uncomfortable just being in the same room as me. While I was grateful to Lili for rustling everyone up, I started to wish she'd waited till I'd left the hospital. I would have preferred a *recovery party* back at home, something both I and the guests could enjoy, rather than this solemn procession of friends and family with nothing to say. Surely Lili knew that?

Once again my mind returned to her farewell of the previous evening. That had pretty much set the tone for today. She had said goodbye to me then, and now it was the turn of my friends and relations.

But there was no need for goodbyes. I wasn't going anywhere. Why didn't any of them get that? I was going to get better. As soon as the docs realised I could hear every word they said, they'd call off the last rites.

Even though I was lying on my back and couldn't move a muscle, I felt exhausted by the end of it all. Just seeing the strained expressions on so many of my loved ones' faces took an unbelievable toll on me. Eventually, though, the whole room cleared until there was just my immediate family left. Then the girls filed out, leaving me alone with Lili once again. But I could tell that even she was getting ready to go home. I'd just been suctioned and cleaned up, so I was surprised to see the door swing open and the doctor who had attended to me most often come back in. He was followed by a colleague I'd never seen before in a white coat.

Lili was standing at the foot of my bed by then, Mustang keys in her hand, but naturally she waited to see what they planned to do to me. Surprisingly, though, the doctors didn't go anywhere near the machines, tubes or pipes. Instead, they walked over to Lili and asked if they could have a word with her.

'Of course,' she replied. 'What about?'

'Rich has been here for two days now,' said the doctor I recognised, 'and, as you know, he's shown no sign of improvement.'

Lili nodded, instinctively looking from him to me.

'Our best guess is that the clot buster has not worked, which means that Rich has less than a two per cent chance of surviving more than a few days.'

He went on to explain that my whole body had shut down, that my internal organs were being kept operational only by electricity and steel, and that my brain had all but switched off because it had been starved of oxygen.

'He can't hear, see, taste, touch, feel or think,' the doctor said, with absolute certainty.

'Okay.' Lili's professional voice was starting to crack, but she just about held it together. 'But what if he does pull through?'

The doctor hesitated before replying. 'If that happens – and it's a very small "if" – then he will still be spending the rest of his life much in this state.' He gestured towards me. 'I'm afraid he'll be little more than a vegetable.'

Lili said nothing for what seemed like minutes. The only noise in the room was the rhythmic sighing and beeping of the machinery that the doctor had just pointed out was keeping me alive. .

'So,' she managed finally, 'what exactly are you saying to me?'

The doctors looked at each other. Then the new one said, 'It's our considered medical opinion that you should consider switching off Rich's life support. I'm sorry, Lili, but he's not coming back.'

Now there was another noise in the room. Or at least in my head. It was me, screaming. These guys in white coats were trying to persuade my wife to kill me. They wanted to pull the plug because they thought I would never recover. They said I was a vegetable, that I would never understand what was going on around me.

But I did understand. In my head, I was the same guy I'd always been. I was the same guy who'd married Lili in 2006. I was the same guy who'd laughed and joked with her over the last three years. I was the same guy ...

I stopped.

I was also the same guy who'd sat down with her early in our marriage and had 'The Conversation' with her. The one about end-of-life scenarios.

I really wish we hadn't done that ...

Lili had brought up the subject, just a couple of months after our wedding. Whatever kinship she and I had felt during our courtship, it had just grown stronger once we were living together. Nights would disappear with one deep conversation after another on every topic under the sun. One particular exchange stayed with me, though. Lili was a practical woman and, through her work in the hospice, she saw the grim side of healthcare on a daily basis. She came home one night and asked if we could talk.

'Sure,' I said. 'What's on your mind?'

'Dying.'

'*Okay* ... What do you mean?'

She told me that she'd just nursed a woman through her final hours, even though the patient had actually died weeks earlier. She had been kept alive by a bank of machines. Every day for weeks, Lili had watched as the woman's family had grown ever more distressed. The sight of their beloved relative tortured them and, when death finally came, it was a relief for everyone.

'Promise me, should the time ever come, that you will never let me become a burden to you,' Lili said. 'If the worst happens, don't throw your life away on an impossible dream. Turn the machines off and move on.'

The picture she described was terrifying, so I had no hesitation in agreeing to her request.

'On one condition, though,' I said. 'You have to swear to do the same for me. I'm eight years older than you. So if anyone's going to end up like that, it's probably me.'

It says a lot about our relationship that this whole life/death conversation took place without any emotion clouding our judgement. We are loving people, but we're practical, too. And now we were prepared for whatever might happen in the future.

But that was then, when we were healthy. A couple of years later, it was a very different story, at least for one of us – and the doctors were waiting for an answer.

I stared at Lili. I already knew what she was going to say. We'd discussed exactly this kind of eventuality and made a solemn pledge to each other. If ever the time came, we'd agreed, we would not hesitate to pull the plug.

Lili opened her mouth to reply.

I wanted to cry.

My own wife was about to kill me.

CHAPTER TEN

Wow. I'm Free

'Don't let them kill me, Lili. I know what we agreed, but I can fight this. I know I can.'

In my head I'm still screaming, but I know nothing's coming out. The three people at the foot of my bed are all staring at me with the same mix of pity and resignation. I've stopped being a person for two of them. I'm just another statistic on the Queen of the Valley charts. I don't know what I am for the third person any more.

'I'm here, Lili! It's still me. Look!'

I watch as she turns to the doctors. She's going to speak. I can scarcely bear to listen. For a second I wish the doctors were right – I wish I didn't have my senses.

Do I really want to hear my wife give the go-ahead for my own death?

She takes a deep breath. The ventilator ensures mine stays the same.

Lili, please …

'This isn't a decision I can make alone,' she says finally. 'I'm going to have to speak to his daughters.'

'Okay, we understand,' the new doctor replies. 'But if you decide to proceed as we suggest, we promise you, he won't feel a thing.'

He pauses, then shrugs helplessly in my direction.

'To all intents and purposes, your husband is already dead.'

A lready dead? What kind of doctor can't tell a living person from a dead one? What sort of a place was this?

I was fuming as Lili kissed me goodbye. How could I be dead if I could hear every word they said? How could I be dead if I could feel my wife's breath and see the tears in her eyes as she leaned towards me?

When her lips touched my face it was like a thousand volts shooting through me.

How could a dead person feel that?

She left with barely a backwards glance. I hoped that was because she was too sad to see me lying there. Realistically, though, I knew it was probably due to guilt. It must be hard to look at the condemned man while you're signing his death warrant.

I didn't care what the nurses did to me after that. I was cleaned, my diaper was changed, my meds were adjusted and my spittle was vacuumed. I let it all happen without thought or embarrassment. They could do what they liked now. After all, in a few hours it wouldn't matter.

Nothing would matter.

I can picture the whole scene.

Shannon, Melanie, Michelle and Lili are sitting around the table at Shannon's house.

'You can't let them switch Dad off.' Melanie is crying.

'But we agreed,' Lili says. 'We made a pact. It's what he would want.'

'But he's our dad,' Shannon says.

'And he's my husband. But even if he recovered, he wouldn't want to live like that. You know he wouldn't.'

The girls nod.

Then Michelle agrees. 'He's always been such an active man. Living like that would be worse than death for him.'

'So it's decided, then,' Lili says. 'I'll tell the doctors tomorrow.'

It was the longest night of my life, knowing that Lili was out there somewhere, probably at Shannon's house with Melanie and Michelle, discussing whether to switch off the machines that were keeping me alive. I ran through every possible permutation of the conversation. Again and again I played the scene in my head, putting different words and arguments in each of their mouths. But every time they reached the same conclusion.

They were going to pull the plug.

Out of sight to my right, the regular sound of the ventilator filling my lungs was a constant reminder of just how bad I was. I needed technology to pee, to breathe, even to stop drowning in my own spit. The doctors were spot on about that. But they'd also said my senses had already shut down. And they couldn't have been more wrong about that.

I was suddenly aware of the National Geographic channel broadcasting away on the TV in front of me.

'Look,' I imagined myself yelling to the doctors, 'I can *see* that. There's nothing wrong with my vision.'

I studied the programme for a few minutes – anything to take my mind off what was about to happen to me. It was a documentary about space. The bright lights on the screen made me want to squint. But I couldn't do that, so I did the next best thing and blinked.

It was a few seconds before I realised the significance of what I'd done.

I just blinked!

My eyes had been opening and shutting involuntarily over the last two days. The lids had been lubricating the balls as normal on autopilot since I'd first woken up. But this time I'd *chosen* to blink. My brain had issued the command and my eyelids had obeyed. Or at least I thought they had. An element of doubt entered my mind. Maybe it was just a coincidence. Maybe I thought of blinking just as my body was about to do it anyway.

There was only one way to find out.

I hadn't tried it for what seemed like ages, although it was probably no more than thirty hours. My mind shifted away from the images on the TV screen. I wasn't interested in what I could *see*. I was only concerned about what I could *control*. I channelled every nerve in my body towards my eyes. I could feel the strain on my mind. If I'd been in control of my own breath, I would have held it to save energy. The only things that mattered at that moment were my eyes.

I counted backwards to three. That seemed appropriate, given the programme on space travel that was still flickering away at the edge of my consciousness.

Three.

Two.

One.

Lift-off.

Darkness!

But this time I knew it wasn't the propofol sending me under. I was still alert. I was still awake. And, for the first time since arriving at the Queen of the Valley, I was truly happy.

All because I'd simply managed to close my eyes.

At least I know it won't come down to a question of money. My medical insurance will take care of everything, I'm confident of that. Cops don't mess around with anything less than full cover and I've paid in plenty over the years.

So what else is there to consider?

Will they think about what I want? What I deserve? Haven't I done enough as a public servant to deserve to live? I'm a teacher, for God's sake. All I want to do is help people. I have a wife and children and grandchildren. You can't just eliminate me. Not like that.

They say I can't live without my ventilator. So what? If you kick a dis-abled man's crutches away, he'll fall over. Does that mean he deserves to die? My ventilator is my crutch.

I'm getting more irate the more I think about it. If I could move my hand I'd pull out all the drips. I'd yank the pipe from my throat. I'd smash the ventilator. And I'd march right out of this building. Who are they to tell me it's time to die?

What did I ever do to them? What harm have I ever done to anyone? It's not my time. Why can't they see that?

It felt so good. So amazing. So . . .

So what?

As I lay there in the darkness I'd created, I was suddenly over-whelmed by another sort of darkness. One moment I'd been in the mood to celebrate my first triumph. My first small step to recovery. The next I couldn't see the point.

So what if I'd managed to shut my eyes? Was that proof I wasn't dying? Was I suddenly qualified to tell stroke experts that they didn't know what they were talking about?

I don't know where the black cloud descended from. Perhaps it was the strain of commanding my own eyes to do my bidding. Perhaps it was the realisation that being able to blink isn't exactly a sign of strength. Either way, for the first time since arriving at The Queen, I felt like I'd had enough. What was the point of fighting something I could not influence? My health insurance guaranteed me the best medical treatment, so if the doctors it paid for said I was as good as dead, they were probably right.

Let's just get the machines switched off and everyone can get on with their life.

I'd changed in such a short space of time from rage to jubilation to acceptance. Who had I been kidding with the self-pity and the gung-ho fighting spirit? My brain being awake wasn't a sign of me being alive. It was a sign of me being in denial.

I finally get it. I'm dying.

My emotions had been all over the place, but they'd settled now on a kind of mellowness I'd never experienced before. Why waste my last hours – or minutes – railing against the world? I just needed to accept my lot and move on. And I needed to let my family move on, too. My functioning senses didn't mean jack. The hearing, the seeing, the touching, the smelling and the tasting might all be working at the moment, despite what the doctors thought, but they would soon be as useless as my arms and legs.

That realisation came as a relief.

Wow. I'm free.

It's amazing how refreshing it feels when you admit you're dying. I repeated the words over and over again in my mind, and it was as though a weight lifted from my supine shoulders.

Stop fighting everything, Rich.

This is what dying feels like. Embrace it.

I couldn't remember being happier. Everything changed at that point. The sounds of my robotic respiratory system were no longer a reminder of how little function my decrepit body had left. They were now the noises of a gadget. A boy's toy. In a heartbeat I went from despising the ventilator's existence to thinking, *This is cool. I don't even have to breathe for myself.*

And my joy only increased when I felt the now familiar whoosh of liquid through my catheter a few minutes later. That was something else I didn't have to worry about. My food arrived via an IV drip, and I got rid of the waste through a plastic pipe in my penis. My breathing was taken care of by a machine, and my spittle was vacuumed up by my own personal attendant. It really was the last word in five-star luxury and I was starting to enjoy it.

The dark mood and the anger were distant memories. Everything was light now. I knew for a fact that death wasn't too bad because, according to the docs, I was as good as dead already. I felt lucky, privileged. I mean, how many people get to die and still see their loved ones? It was just a question of making the most of my remaining moments. When Lili returned I wouldn't take my eyes off her for a second.

When I go, I want her to be the last thing I see ...

I looked once more at the TV. The space-exploration programme had finished and images of fish and coral now filled the screen. The soundlessness of the underwater film reminded me of my own situation.

But not for long. Not for long ...

CHAPTER ELEVEN

I Think There's Someone in There

I'm awake.

It's dark, so it must be nighttime.

Or is it?

I open my eyes.

Neat.

I'd forgotten I could do that. I want to do it again. So I do.

Blink. Blink. Blink.

It's slower than I'm used to, but there's no denying who is in control. These aren't spasms or reflexes. It's me. I'm blinking my own eyes.

If I conquer Everest next year that won't give me more pleasure than achieving this.

I see the nurse leaning over to siphon my mouth. I blink at her. She doesn't respond. Why would she? She must have seen me blink a thousand times. How is she expected to know that this is the real deal? That this is me.

It's my own fault. I'm the boy who blinked wolf.

I could hear the buzz of activity outside the door. There was traffic noise coming in through the open window, too. Both were signs that the new day had begun. I knew it wouldn't be long before the men in white coats came in to see me.

I wondered when Lili would arrive with the permission they needed. I desperately wanted to speak to her. Whatever angst she was putting herself through had to be stopped. I was still fine about dying. I figured it was barely a short hop across to the other side from where I was now. What's the worst that could happen when you're virtually dead already?

Did I even need to see her again? It would have been lovely, of course. But she'd already said goodbye to me. And, in my own way, I'd said as much back to her. As for all my family and friends, the thirty or forty people who'd packed the waiting room yesterday, they hadn't needed to say anything. Their presence spoke volumes. Our business was done. None of them expected to see me again.

I lost track of time, as usual. For me, the day didn't start until Lili arrived. The only difference on this day was that I knew the second she walked through the door it would be the last time I saw her do that. A couple of days, or even hours, earlier that thought would have shaken me to the core. But I was okay about it now. The first step in solving a problem is admitting you have one. And I'd admitted I was dying. Whatever Lili had to say during our final meeting would just speed me even more contentedly on my way.

I guessed she'd had to pass through reception on her way in. And reception had tipped off the medics. Or maybe it was just a coincidence. Either way, seconds after she'd strolled in, hunched over like Atlas with the whole weight of the world on her shoulders, the two doctors from the night before arrived too.

They each went about their business, checking readings and charts and IV bags. Then, finally, one of them spoke.

'So, Mrs Marsh, have you had a chance to consider what we spoke about yesterday?'

She nodded.

Here we go. This is it. How long have I got? Ten minutes? Maybe thirty, by the time they get everything ready?

Lili coughed quietly. 'Richard's daughters and I, we have decided ...' She paused. I could tell she was choking up. She cleared her throat again and continued: 'We have decided that we don't want to turn off the machines. We want to give him a chance.'

No, Lili. It's all right. You don't need to do this. I'm ready. I'm ready to go.

The doctors looked at each other.

Eventually, one of them said, 'If that's what you want, Lili.'

'It is.' She turned to look into my eyes. 'I can't turn him off. It's not right. He's still with us. I can feel it.'

I didn't know what to make of that. How could she 'feel' I was still there? That was confusing. And she'd already said goodbye to me. So was she just saying anything to delay making the final decision? I actually felt disappointed. What was the point of carrying on? From the looks on the doctors' faces, Lili's decision was just postponing the inevitable. I'd maybe have a few more days with my family, if I were lucky. Then nature would take its course, by which time my hearing and my eyesight and everything else would have gone the same way as my lungs and my bladder. It was just a matter of time.

Lili had made the best choice she could according to her conscience, but that wouldn't keep me alive any longer.

The two doctors are obviously disappointed. I can only imagine they feel sorry for me. They have nothing to gain by pulling the plug. Apart from freeing up an ICU bed, I suppose. But it's not their job to worry about logistics. The Queen has a whole admin department to deal with that sort of thing.

Lili is on the verge of tears. Even though she's given me a stay of execution, she knows I'm on the final straight. She can stop my life being taken prematurely, but she can't keep me alive indefinitely.

While I continue to watch my wife I don't take much notice of the lead doctor as he comes over and begins to examine my face closely. It's as if he's trying to peer into my soul. As he leans in closer I can't help myself. I blink.

He walks back to his colleague, has a quick word, then leaves the room. A few minutes later he returns. Then a man I recognise as the neurologist who treated me in the Emergency Room arrives.

'I understand you want a second opinion,' he says.

The lead doctor nods, and gestures towards me. 'Let us know what you think.'

The neurologist comes over and studies my face with the same intensity as the doctor had done. He cocks his head, like a dog listening for the sound of a rabbit.

'Okay, can I try something?' he calls over to the doctors.

'Go ahead,' they answer in unison.

He takes a deep breath, then says, 'Rich, I think you might be able to hear me. If you can, blink once for yes.'

I watch his mouth shape the words, I smell his breath as he says them. Finally, I hear them.

Or at least I think I do.

Did he just address me directly? Little old me?

I'm so stunned I almost forget to respond.

Come on, eyes. We can do this . . .

I concentrate as hard as I can and manage to blink.

The neurologist smiles. 'Okay,' he says. 'Let's try something else. Rich, if you can understand me, now blink twice.'

I get it. He's worried it was just a coincidence the first time.

I blink twice.

At the foot of my bed Lili and the two doctors are staring at me in silence.

The neurologist turns to them, and even though he's now at the edge of my vision I can tell his smile is as wide as his belt.

'Ladies and gentlemen,' he says, 'I think there's someone in there.'

Straight ahead of me, Lili starts to cry.

CHAPTER TWELVE

Blink Once for Yes

'Hello, Richard. I'm Dr Kako.'

The man I've seen so many times before – the man who has been test-ing me and checking my progress – is introducing himself as though we've never met. And, in a way, we never have. He has no idea I've been watching him like a hawk for three days. I've no clue how many coma patients he's seen in his career, or how many people in a vegetative state. But I'm guess-ing it's a lot. He diagnosed me immediately. Then all his colleagues agreed with his assessment. Every single piece of medical evidence pointed to that conclusion. It's not his fault that on this occasion he was wrong.

'Can you blink if you can hear me?'

I blink.

'That's great, Rich. It's so good to meet you.'

I blink again.

He smiles.

'I'd like to try to explain what you're going through, if that's okay. You have a condition called locked-in syndrome.'

It's the first time in my life I've ever heard that phrase.

Lili, now standing out of my field of vision to the side, says, 'I've never heard of that.'

So it's a new one for an experienced medical professional, too. That goes some way to explaining why the doctors didn't arrive at the correct diagnosis sooner.

Dr Kako begins to tell me, as clearly as he can, what has happened to me. The blood clot on my basilar artery was preventing oxygen reaching my brain. They'd given me the clot buster, with my permission, to try to break it down. But I'd shown no signs of improvement, so they'd assumed it hadn't worked. In fact, in the hours after the injection, my body had continued to shut down rather than improve. In 99 per cent of similar cases, brain function is the next thing to go. All senses cease working and the patient slips into a vegetative state. The doctor explains that I had exhibited every single symptom for a coma. For more than two days, the only person who could possibly have known I wasn't in one was me.

'But the blinking changed everything,' he says with a smile.

Wow. It's a lot to take in. Imagine if I hadn't suddenly been able to control my blinking. They'd still think I was comatose. Imagine if Lili had given them permission to shut me down when the doctors had first recommended it. I could have done nothing to show them I was still here.

How lucky am I?

I don't know who else would describe me as lucky. Watching Dr Kako's expression, I get the distinct impression he would pick other adjectives. As he continues to talk, I start to understand why.

'It gives me no pleasure to tell you that around ninety per cent of locked-in patients die within the first four months of being diagnosed.'

Okay ...

'And of those who survive, the majority never regain any motor control.' He pauses. 'By that I mean it's unlikely you'll ever be able to move your limbs or your head or control your body. So there's a very high chance you'll never be able to talk, either.'

I have to admire his honesty. I would hate to deliver this kind of speech

to anyone. It reminds me of all the occasions I was the bearer of bad news
as a cop. All those times I knocked on a front door knowing that what I had
to say would ruin the lives of the people behind it. I know how hard that
is, which is why I know this doctor is doing an excellent job.

I want to tell him it's all right. A few hours ago I made my peace with
myself. I was prepared for death. Nothing has changed since then. If it hap-
pens, it happens. But at least I won't go down alone. And I won't go down
quietly. I'm going to fight this. For one very good reason.

I hear Lili cough.

There's no way of saying what I'm thinking through blinks. But she
knows.

'Is it you, Rich? Are you really in there?'
    Lili was standing over me, both of her hands wrapped
around one of mine.

I blinked once.

'Is it blink once for "yes"?' She looked over to the doctor for
confirmation.

'Whatever you agree with Richard,' he said. 'Let's assume it is,
though. That's how I've been talking to him. Okay, Richard?'

I blinked again.

'Oh, Rich!'

Whenever we talked long into the night, I usually couldn't
wait to get my point across. I was so eager to keep the conversation
going, to hear Lili's response to whatever had just popped into my
mind, that I would blurt it out in a flood of words before she'd
even finished speaking. But now I was happy just to listen to her –
and talking to me, no about me. After so much time with her sitting silently alongside me, her voice was as refreshing as a cool
beer on a hot day.

She fired a stream of questions at me and I did my best to

reply. But until you try it, you don't realise how tricky it is to conduct a conversation with someone by asking them only 'yes/no' questions. More than anything else, Lili wanted to know 'How do you feel?' Try answering that with one blink or two. After a while, we both started to find it funny.

Much worse than being asked questions I couldn't answer was hearing Lili tell me she was sorry for not realising sooner. I wished I could tell her it wasn't her fault. In fact, I was only alive because of her. If she had left the decision to the men in the white coats, the machines would have been switched off already.

Speaking of whom, my care routine wasn't about to change just because everyone now knew I was 'awake'. The only difference was, whenever a nurse announced it was time for me to rest – usually after about an hour of consciousness – she told me first, *then* Lili, before turning the lever on the IV drip.

What does it all mean for me?

On a practical level, I guess it means they can't switch off my machines now. I am alive, and I have full cognitive function. I may be paralysed but I'm not brain-dead. I'm just trapped in a body that isn't working. Morally, I'm as entitled to life as anyone else in the room.

Beyond that, there's something greater, especially in the immediate term. I can communicate. With my wife, my daughters, my friends – and my medical team.

When he was first explaining my condition, Dr Kako told me, 'You can now make decisions about your own care.'

But I don't know what those decisions might be. After all, Dr Kako is part of the team who have told me I have a very low chance of survival.

As usual, I woke up without anyone noticing. The anyone in this instance was more than Lili and the nurse. Shannon and Melanie were back as well. I guessed by their anxious faces that they'd heard the news. They were both staring at me, waiting for some sort of sign, but they didn't flinch when I woke up, so my eyes must have been open already. Perhaps they'd tried to speak to me earlier and got no response. That would have been heartbreaking for them.

I needed to get their attention. Blinking was all I had, so that was what I did.

Blink. Blink. Blink.

Nothing.

Blinkblinkblinkblinkblinkblinkblink.

Finally, Lili noticed.

'I think he's woken up,' she said.

Seconds later, my daughters were crowding around my bed.

'Dad, are you awake?'

It was Melanie's tentative voice. She sounded small and young. Nerves, I imagined.

I blinked again and felt a slight ache in my eyes. It's surprising how tiring blinking can be when it's all you can do.

The smiles on all three women's faces were a picture. The girls looked at each other, then both spoke at once. Neither managed a 'yes/no' question, so Lili explained what they had to do.

The pleasure I'd felt from seeing Lili earlier was trebled as I watched all three of them get a kick out of just talking to me. An hour must have flown by, because suddenly the nurse asked if I needed a rest.

Blink. Blink.

She gave me the sort of look that brooks no argument.

'Well, I think you do,' she said. Then she announced to the others that I'd be able to pick up the conversations after my nap.

In sixty years I can't remember ever having an itch on my elbow before. Yet that was the sensation I felt throughout last night. This morning it had shifted and felt like gnats figure-skating on my knee. Both times I thought I was going to go mad as I lay there without the ability to scratch, or even the ability to ask someone to scratch it for me.

Neither itch, though, was as excruciating as what I'm going through now. Somehow, inexplicably, for the first time in my life, I have an itch on the big toe of my left foot. If I didn't know better, I would think one of Melanie's boys is down there with a feather.

I can feel the propofol and morphine doing their work, trying to send me to sleep as per the nurse's instruction. I can feel my body giving in to it. My mind is hanging on at the moment but it won't for long. It doesn't matter. I'm used to it now. When the cloud descends there's no point in fighting it.

And yet, I want to scratch that toe so much. Just once, before I go under, I want to rub it against its neighbour and end the torment. I put everything I've got into trying.

I try again. And again, as the drugs take hold.

Just once more, one more giant push. One more …

Waking up again, for at least the third time that day, was another happy experience. After the initial sense of confusion, a thrill surged through me as I remembered I'd been conversing with my family. I was happy to see them jump to their feet with the same degree of pleasure when they realised I was back in the room.

That was the biggest positive for me overall – knowing that I wasn't a piece of furniture in the corner. I was alive. I was a human being. People weren't talking across me any more. I was *back in the room.*

Even with communication restored, though, there were only so much that could be said. However pleased my family were to see me, they chose not to mention – and I was unable to bring up – some undeniable truths.

I wasn't brain-dead. I was conscious and alert. But I had no motor skills and the experts were almost certain that I would never regain them. The situation I found myself in at that moment – propped up in a bed, plugged into machines and intravenous bags delivering nutrition and medication – was unlikely to change. What Lili and the girls were looking at now was probably what they'd be looking at in a year's time.

Assuming I lived that long. Dr Kako's best guess had been four months. That was the average life expectancy of a patient diagnosed with locked-in syndrome. But the thing about averages, of course, is that you can be much higher or much lower. In other words, I might have four months, but I might equally have eight months – or two weeks. There was only one way to find out.

As I lay there, doing my best to answer my girls' questions, I was determined to cling onto the sense of acceptance I'd felt the night before.

I had to, because nothing had changed. I hadn't been saved. They'd all just caught up with where I already was. I was still on the critical list. I was still in an ICU bed. I still couldn't control any part of my body, except for my eyelids. I was still going to die.

And, in the meantime, what? What quality of life would I have? Could I imagine eight months of this? Just lying there, watching my loved ones run out of things to say to me. We'd all know why they were there. They'd be counting down the days till they didn't have to come any more.

That wasn't fair. It wasn't what I wanted for any of them. My children had the rest of their lives ahead of them. Lili, as well, was too young to be saddled with the responsibility of keeping my spirits up while my body slipped slowly to the grave. They all had jobs, children, lives they should be getting on with. I didn't want them to sacrifice any more than they already had for me. But how could I tell them that?

Another enforced nap, another round of conversations, and another fruitless attempt to scratch the itch on my big toe passed before I hit on an idea. I would have to use the only power I had. Play the one card I held.

I would stop blinking.

If I did that, they would think I'd gone. Communicating with my eyes was how I was telling them I was still alive. If I stopped doing that, eventually the doctors would have no choice. They'd convince Lili that I'd gone and persuade her to switch off the machines. It would break my heart to leave them, but it would be far worse to watch them throw their lives away in order to look after me.

In the meantime, though, I still had some questions to answer. Whatever Melanie and Shannon came up with, I listened and responded. Only when they'd all left for the night did I think again about my plan. Did I reply to my last yes/no? Did I have the final word?

Yes, I did.

There was no other option available to me. My body was showing no sign of coming back on line. It would never repair itself. I was buried in sand with the tide coming in and no part of my body was going to dig me out.

This is it. This is the end. There is nothing left for me here any more.

Then I saw the sheet above my left foot begin to move and all thoughts of death went straight out of the window.

CHAPTER THIRTEEN

T. H. A. N. K. Y. O. U.

'No change given.'

I'm scrabbling around in my pocket for the correct coins. The light on the vending machine is taunting me to get it right. I count up the quarters and dimes in my palm, then study the glass panel. What can I afford?

Everything looks so good.

The cafeteria is empty apart from me. There are no patients, no nurses, no visiting relatives. I can take my time.

Shall I try something new or go with an old favourite? Decisions, decisions.

Finally, I make my choice. I place the coins into the slot and listen as they crash down into the box below. None of them is rejected, which is a relief.

I press the chunky buttons on the front.

'F' followed by '6'.

There's a short delay before the mechanised whirr tells me something is happening. I watch through the glass as F6 glides to the end of the line, then drops into the trough below. I push my hand through the trapdoor and retrieve my prize.

Yum, another lovely serving of morphine and propofol.

Nighttime was the worst. Having Lili and the girls and my friends around during the day really kept my spirits up. We settled into a routine of conversing when we wanted to, not because we felt we had to. But then, at the end of every day, when they all left, I realised how much more I wanted to say.

The weird thing was, it wasn't so much their company I missed. It was their protection. I knew I was in the finest medical facility that money could buy, and I had no complaints about the staff at the Queen of the Valley or any of their procedures. But lying there, unable to move, unable to speak, I just felt so damn vulnerable. When you're six foot two and you can bench-press your own body weight and you've spent most of your working life with a gun and a badge, it's easy to forget what fear feels like. I'd always been a physical guy and I could still handle myself – right up to the morning of the stroke. But now I was completely at the mercy of others.

The doctors and nurses and ancillary teams were all great. But they were still strangers. My years on the force had taught me the value of back-up. Now Lili and the girls were my back-up. They wouldn't let anything happen to me.

Even weirder than feeling intimidated in an environment that was designed to help me was the realisation that it was getting worse. I hadn't been scared at all the night when I'd first accepted I was dying. I'd made my peace with Lili, the Almighty and the world. I was content.

Now, though, I realised I didn't want to die, which in turn forced me to acknowledge just how feeble my grip on life actually was. My sense of helplessness had driven me to consider stopping blinking so as not to prolong my family's agony, and I'd been happy to make that decision. But then my toe had moved, and it was as though I could make out the flickering of a beacon somewhere in the distance. It gave me hope, but it was incredibly faint. The slightest mistake might snuff it out. I still had so much to live for, but I didn't have the strength to do it on my own. I needed Lili's support to get me through this. So when she left me alone each night I felt utterly defenceless.

Dr Kako and his team were surprised by the movement in my toe, but less excited than I'd expected them to be. At least at first. They'd initially interpreted my blinking – correctly – as just nerve endings twitching involuntarily, and they came to a similar conclusion about my toe now. Just another muscle spasm, they suspected. The only way to prove it was under my control was for Dr Kako to ask me to move it, and then wait for a response.

An interesting half an hour later and he finally conceded that his initial diagnosis had been incorrect.

'That's great, Richard. You're making progress.'

For a second it felt like being released from jail, but my hopes were almost immediately dashed. The professionals still seemed far from convinced that my 'progress' was anything to shout about.

Didn't my twitching toe indicate that my entire body was waking up? Or did they think it was just the valiant last action of a dying man?

They've already told me how rare locked-in syndrome is. Maybe they don't know where we go from here, either.

Either way, my girls weren't about to let reality get in the way of optimism. They brought in a large collection of photographs of the whole family and took it in turns to hold them up in front of me. It was great seeing photos of them as kids and all the other important people from my past. My life was literally flashing in front of my eyes.

After we'd looked at everything, Shannon mounted the photos onto a board and placed it on the dresser – below the TV. And in front of the mirror. They had no way of knowing what a relief that was. At some point someone had turned the mirror towards me, which had forced me to look at myself all day long. And that was something I just didn't want to do.

But now I was faced with an even worse situation. It took me a couple of seconds to realise that Melanie was holding a camera in her hand. I knew she just wanted to celebrate what they all considered an upturn in my fortunes, but if I couldn't bear to see my face in a mirror, I certainly didn't want a permanent reminder of how I looked.

How could I stop her? I had no way of telling her anything other than 'yes' or 'no', so I used the only tools available to me. I blinked repeatedly and I wiggled my toe until I thought it might fall off. On anyone else this frenzied activity would have been considered no more than a couple of nervous twitches. On me, I imagine it looked like a seismic explosion.

Lili noticed first.

'Are you trying to tell us something?' she asked me.

Blink. Just the one now that I'd got her attention.

She turned to the girls. 'What could it be?' she asked, wondering what had suddenly changed. 'Is it the camera?'

Holding it up, Melanie shrugged. 'Are you okay with me taking your picture, Dad?'

Blink. Blink.

'That's a definite no,' Lili said.

Thank you, darling.

I don't think they understood what my problem was, but it meant the world to me that they listened.

Thank God for my back-up …

I'm sweating. That's what it feels like, anyway. And my heart is racing. Again, that's what it feels like. But the noises coming from my ventilator are as regular as ever. Does it know that I've just been dreaming?

Legend has it that nightmares can be induced by eating cheese late at night. A lot of people believe that. But a block of cheddar isn't in the same league as propofol. I wake up so terrified that I'm surprised to see I'm not sitting bolt upright.

Seeing my past appearing before my eyes in a series of photographs was one thing. But I was determined to see my future as well. However long I had left, I intended to make the most of it.

The next few days passed in a slow blur. Shannon had to get back to her job and look after her family, but she came by whenever she could. Lili managed to arrange compassionate leave with the hospice, and Melanie said she would stay as long as I wanted her to. She was still bunking at Shannon's place. Only Michelle had left. She kissed me goodbye before returning to Alabama to take care of her family and her job.

Various friends continued to visit, too. The atmosphere in the room was much lighter than it had been on the second day. There wasn't quite an air of jubilation, but certainly the fact that everyone knew I could hear them made a big difference. They didn't feel like they were shouting into a void, performing to an empty auditorium. More than one or two of my early visitors had clearly been uncomfortable with just hearing the sound of their own voice. Now, though, their true personalities had an opportunity to shine.

Lili and Melanie did their best to keep my spirits up, but in truth they didn't really need to do anything. From the moment my toe had come back on line I'd been hopeful that other parts of my body would follow. And I didn't have too long to wait.

Just after Lili had left one morning a nurse came in, said 'hello', then moved round to check on my switches and dials. Next she walked the entire length of my bed and back round the other side in order to check my pillows were suitably plumped. As I casually watched her over my left shoulder I realised something was different. It took me a few seconds to figure out what it was. Then it hit me.

I haven't seen my left shoulder since the stroke.

Without me noticing, my eyes had regained the power to rotate. I had to test it immediately, so I zinged my gaze from left to right, ceiling to floor, repeatedly. My field of vision had suddenly increased enormously.

Before long, the nurse noticed what was happening and asked if I was doing it intentionally. When she was satisfied that I was, she called in Dr Kako.

'Can you look to the left, Richard?'

Despite the weirdness of having to make my eyeballs do it, I looked to the left.

'Great. How about up?'

Again, I concentrated on doing just that.

'Okay. Now, how about left, then right?'

I looked left, then right.

The doctor smiled. 'I think you'll find your life will be a whole lot easier from now on.'

I wondered why that would be. Did he mean that the eyes were a clue that everything else would suddenly spark back into life, too? I doubted it. No one was exactly popping the champagne corks. So what was the big deal about my eyes regaining their ability to move?

Little did I know it, but before long I would have the answer. Because I would be able to ask the question.

I don't think I'll ever get used to drifting in and out of sleep during the daytime. I'm not sure my family will, either. Half the time they don't know whether I'm awake or not. Sometimes I come round with Lili or Melanie in mid-question. Even though I can now control their movement, my eyes still open without any instruction from me.

Sometimes I come round and it's so foggy I think I'm still dreaming.

Today I'm sure I'm awake but there's a complete stranger in the room asking my family to follow her. Is she real? I've certainly never seen her before. Is she taking them to the medicine vending machine I dreamed of in the cafeteria?

It'll be interesting to see what she brings back . . .

The stranger was standing next to me.

'Hello, Richard,' she said. 'My name is Susan. I'm your speech therapist.'

Okay, that clears it up. I'm definitely dreaming. Why would someone with a hose down their throat and no control over their mouth need a speech therapist?

It was as though she heard me.

'Later on, I hope to be able to help you speak again,' she explained. 'But for now I just want to start with another way of communicating which, Dr Kako tells me, you are now ready for.'

What could I possibly be ready for?

Unless she was going to teach me semaphore using a tiny flag glued to my big toe, I couldn't see what she had in mind. I looked to Lili in the hope that she might interpret my thoughts and share them with Susan. Interestingly, I noticed she was smiling. Melanie was, too. And these were not the putting-on-a-brave-face smiles that hospital visitors routinely practise. They both looked genuinely happy.

'So, Richard,' Susan said, 'have you ever seen one of these before?'

She held up a white board, about the size of an A4 sheet of paper, divided into five sections. In each corner there was a sequence of letters and in the middle a blank space.

Blink. Blink.

'Okay, this is known as a spell board. But you can think of it as your hotline to your family.'

She was making so little sense that I was tempted to close my eyes. That was my ultimate weapon. But I decided to go along with it even though a hotline, as far as I could remember, was a telephone. And I was sure I would not be using one of them for a long time. In fact, I had already come to terms with the prospect that I may never make a call again.

Undeterred, Susan started to explain how the spell board worked. She did this by asking me to choose a short word.

Bike.

My Harley was something else I would probably never experience again.

'Have you chosen?'

Blink.

'Okay, now I'm going to hold the spell board in front of you and I want you to move your eyes and find the first letter of that word.'

I looked at the top-left section. The letters there ran from A to F.

'Are you looking at this corner?' Susan asked, following my gaze to the top-left section and tapping it with her finger.

Blink.

'Okay, good. Now I'm going to run through these letters and when I get to the one you're thinking of, I want you to blink.'

Blink.

'A,' she said, and paused.

'B.'

Blink.

'B?'

Blink.

'Great. Now I'm going to write that letter down in the central section of the board.'

Once she'd done that, we moved on to the second, third and fourth letters. It was a slow process but by the end I could see my word – bike – staring back at me. A few minutes earlier, that word had been locked in my head. Now, without uttering a single sound, I had managed to transfer it onto the board in front of me. Which meant it was now in the head of everyone else in the room, too.

I've just spoken for the first time!

When I'd woken up that morning I'd had no idea that the day would turn out so special. Second only to the trauma of not being able to move is that of not being able to speak. But now, thanks to this simple piece of hardboard and a pen, I could convey my thoughts to my wife and children again. It was truly amazing. An absolute highlight of my life. So simple and yet so utterly life-changing. When Susan asked me to try a longer word, there was only one choice.

T. H. A. N. K. Y. O. U.

I didn't think I'd ever met a speech therapist before. I'd certainly never seen one cry. But Susan and Lili, I realised, were both choking back tears. I hadn't meant to cause that. I'd just wanted to express my sincere gratitude.

Have you never been thanked by a locked-in survivor before?

When our time was up, Susan – composed and professional again now – congratulated me on a good first session and said she'd leave the spell board behind. Lili couldn't wait to have a con-versation – Susan had trained her and Melanie while I'd been asleep – but I had a more pressing need. The first words I spelled out after 'hello' were 'I'm hot.'

'You're hot?'

I watched as Lili instinctively pulled her top to her. Clearly she wasn't feeling the heat.

'Do you want me to get you a fan?'

Blink.

'Okay, then. Now, how are you feeling after that session?'

There were so many other things I could – and should – have spelled out at that moment, but only one thought came to my mind.

T. I. R. E. D.

I'm sure I saw Lili deflate just a little. She was eager for some quality time and I'd served up a conversational cul-de-sac. But I couldn't help it. I was absolutely shattered.

All I'd done was shift my gaze in different directions for half an hour but it felt like I'd just finished an Iron Man. For the first time since arriving in the ICU I felt totally spent. My eyes, I sup-posed, were parts of my physical being. And as they were virtually all I could control, it made some sense that all of me was exhausted from the effort.

But I wasn't only suffering physically. I was completely over-whelmed by the mental and especially the emotional exertion. All I was doing was spelling out simple words, but it was taking every-thing I had. I was so tired that even my newfound optimism started to ebb away. I'd been given a lifeline to the real world, but how long would it last? Was this a genuine glimmer of hope or merely the final act of a dying man?

E. V. E. N. I. F. I. A. S. K. T. H. E. Q. U. E. S. T. I. O. N. D. O. E. S. A. N. Y. B. O. D. Y. R. E. A. L. L. Y. K. N. O. W. T. H. E. A. N. S. W. E. R.?

CHAPTER FOURTEEN

What's the Catch?

What if I had never learned how to blink? What if I had never recovered the ability to move my eyes from side to side? Where would I be now? It's days since Lili said she didn't want to turn off my life support. How long would she have kept that up? How many times can you come into a room and sit next to a body that is one off switch away from being a corpse?

The spelling board enriched my life to a degree that no one on the outside could have comprehended. For a start, it meant I now had a fan aimed at my face. Yet, in less than a day, I was already starting to view that as an infuriating symbol of my helplessness. Moving my eyes had been a massive breakthrough, especially as it had come so soon after I had regained control of my toe. But as another twenty-four hours passed, I was disappointed that nothing else showed any sign of activity. No more toes, no fingers, I couldn't move my tongue or even sniff. My recovery seemed to have ground to a halt almost as soon as it had begun.

What was it the medics had said when they first diagnosed me with locked-in syndrome? Ninety per cent of sufferers never regain their motor skills. Had I been fooling myself by thinking the toe and the eyes were the start of a full recovery? What if they were nothing of the sort?

What if they are all I'm ever going to get back?

I wished I had something more common, something the medical profession had been able to research in depth. Of course, Lili had been trawling the internet ever since my diagnosis in the hope of finding some literature on how she and the family should respond to living with this scenario, but the information online was not only clinically focused but scarce and contradictory. Which perhaps explained why my own medical team seemed so foxed. They weren't predicting how my recovery might progress. They were responding to it.

So I decided there was no point spelling out the question that was burning me up inside. I wanted to be told the truth about my condition, and up to that point I was confident I had been. But if I asked whether I'd ever be able to speak again, or stand, or walk, I figured the medical team would have to admit they didn't know. And that was not something I wanted to hear. In any case, using the spell board was still unimaginably draining. If I thought I could do without it in a conversation, I usually tried, and went back to blinking instead.

Despite my fears, I soon realised that the doctors had not given up on me. I didn't know whether they'd got in touch with a locked-in syndrome expert or had been scouring the medical journals, but a week after I'd arrived in the ICU Dr Kako announced, 'We'd like to talk about our plans for you. Are you okay with that?'

I blinked once.

The medical team had said I would always be consulted about any big decisions, but this was the first time that had happened since the conversation about the clot buster. Mentally, I braced myself. I had no idea what Dr Kako was going to say.

'We've been monitoring your diaphragm. We think it's showing signs of wanting to work again.'

'Wanting to'? What does that mean?

'If you could start breathing on your own, you could come off life support,' he continued, anticipating my question. 'It will be the first stage to claiming back your body.'

Sounds great. What's the catch?

'There are downsides, of course.' I started to wonder if he could read my mind. 'We don't know when your diaphragm will kick in, and if we were to test it now, that would involve removing your breathing tube from your windpipe. You would be without air for a few moments, and then hopefully the lungs would start filling naturally. But if they didn't, we would have to reinsert the pipe.' His expression was pure sympathy. 'You would need to be conscious during such a procedure, and I can't promise it wouldn't hurt.'

So what's the alternative?

'The other option is to put you under, remove the tube from your mouth while you're asleep, and perform a tracheotomy. That involves making an incision in your throat in the little indentation just below your Adam's apple. We would then open that up and insert a small tube – about a quarter of an inch in diameter – down your windpipe. The tube has a little balloon on it which seals off your windpipe so you can't breathe through your nose or mouth. So you'll still be breathing via the ventilator at first, but it will be much easier for us to test the strength of your lungs if we go with this method.'

Then, if my diaphragm proved strong enough, they could remove the tube and the balloon very easily, which would allow me to breathe normally again.

The doctor gave me a few moments to think about the two alternatives, but I'd already made up my mind.

Eventually, he asked, 'Okay, Richard, is there anything more I can tell you?'

Blink. Blink.

'Great. So, do you think you would like to go ahead with the tracheotomy?'

Blink.

'Just to confirm. You would like to go ahead?'

'Blink.'

'Okay, that's decided.'

As I watched Dr Kako run his usual checks over my vital signs I felt proud of myself for having made a decision. Psychologically, that was a significant milestone. Everything else since the clot buster had been decided by other people. This time, only one person had had a say – and that person was me.

Yet, as soon as the doctor left the room, I was overwhelmed by conflicting emotions. On the one hand, the offer of a tracheotomy seemed to prove that the doctors thought I was making progress. But on the other, they were suggesting cutting my throat open and inserting another tube. Whichever way I looked at it, that seemed extreme. Should I be worried? Did they know what they were doing? How many locked-in victims had they treated before me? Was I a patient to them or an exciting research opportunity?

I don't want to be a guinea pig.

There was a third element to consider, too. Who was to say that my lungs would begin working again? The doctors didn't know. I didn't know. I'd already beaten enormous odds just by regaining the movement in my eyes and my toe, so I was sure to be a test case. There were no rules about what would happen next.

What if a surgeon removed all my tubes and I couldn't breathe? Would they even be able to tell? I could suffocate before anyone realised.

Even as I was being given the anaesthetic, those doubts were still swimming around my mind. In fact, as I drifted into blackout, I was wondering whether I had made a serious mistake.

Thankfully, the second I awoke I knew the operation had been a success. Despite the painkillers that were being pumped into my body, I could feel the tube penetrating my neck. But even though the rubber block had been removed from my mouth, not only could I still smell and taste it: I thought I could feel it, too. My jaw, I was told, was now clamped shut, so why did it still ache like it was being wedged open like an annoying swing door in the breeze?

I'd ask that question on my spell board as soon as I had the energy. At that moment, I just needed to calm down and accept the latest phase of my treatment. I needed to be positive. The pipe down my throat had gone. The comforting wheeze of the ventilator remained, though.

I wonder what will happen when they try switching it off.

It would be two days before I found out.

There's so much I want to ask. So many questions. Where do I start? Or should I just conserve my energy? I'm not out of the woods yet, I know that. And there's no point asking questions if I'm not going to like the answers.

I'd thought coming off the ventilator would be the next big challenge. I was wrong. Even though I was breathing through a different tube now, nothing else had changed. I was still plumbed into the same machine and spittle was still building up in my mouth and throat. Which meant I still needed to be suctioned.

I'd got used to the little pipe vacuuming my mouth. It was disconcerting rather than uncomfortable or painful. Like any visit to the dentist, the sound of the tool bursting into life was often worse than the treatment itself. During the suctioning itself my mind would often drift off somewhere else. I assumed that would continue under this new arrangement. Unfortunately, my body had other ideas.

The suctioning was done hourly or bi-hourly, day and night. Much of the time I didn't even notice it because the nurses tried to do it while I was asleep. But shortly after I'd woken up to find the pipe sticking out of my throat a nurse walked through the door and headed straight for where the suction pump was kept.

She had attended to me dozens of times since I'd arrived in the ICU and had always been friendly and careful, even before I'd been diagnosed with locked-in syndrome. In fact, she hadn't really needed to alter her behaviour once that had happened, because she'd addressed me directly right from the start. As usual, she was smiling with her mouth and eyes as she leaned across me, suction pump in hand.

'Okay, Richard, you know what time it is.'

Blink.

In truth, though, that was all I knew. I fully expected the usual, familiar procedure. But when the nurse started fiddling with my trach pipe, I immediately realised something had changed.

I gasped as the pipe was pulled from my throat. That was the only way I could breathe.

What the hell is she playing at?

Actually, I didn't gasp at all. I couldn't. I didn't even have the strength for that. So much for hoping my diaphragm would kick in. The whole operation had been a complete waste of time – and now it was becoming terrifying as well.

The hole that had been cut into my neck was obviously kept open via a kind of stopper. The second the respiratory tube came out, the incision stayed open and I felt another tube slide down in its place. Then, somewhere deep inside my windpipe, I felt – and heard – the buzz of the tiny vacuum cleaner as it siphoned up all the liquid that had collected there.

'Nearly there,' the nurse said.

It must have been only a few seconds later, but by then I'd lost track of time completely. The pump sounded worse than it felt, but the real pain was due to not being able to breathe. It felt like someone had wrapped a polythene bag over my head – someone who was smiling broadly while they held it tight.

You're killing me.

To my right, the familiar sound of the ventilator taunted me, pushing out breaths that were no longer reaching me. In and out, in and out.

Just plug me back in. Please!

I was burning inside. My lungs felt like they were going to burst. I couldn't believe this was the only way to clear my throat of spittle. Why hadn't Dr Kako warned me about this when he'd explained the pros and cons of the tracheotomy? Given the choice of drowning or suffocating while a smiling assassin did some vacuuming, at that moment I would have taken my chances with the former. At least that was the work of my own body.

'There we go. All done.'

It was over. The sucking stopped and the pipe was withdrawn. The scrape of plastic on plastic as the nurse pulled it through the stopper turned my stomach. Then I suffered the same sensation as she reinserted the breathing pipe. But almost immediately I couldn't care less. The first puff of oxygen hitting my lungs was pure nectar from the gods. It was the closest thing I could imagine to a natural high. For a second I felt like the luckiest man alive. And why? Because I could breathe again, the most basic activity of a normal human being.

But I'm not a normal human being any more, am I? And I'm not sure I ever will be again.

If I hadn't admitted it to myself before, I couldn't escape from it now.

Where's my spell board? How long would it take me to spell out 'stop'? Too long. A minute, at least. They could kill me in half that time. I need to work out something else. A safe word. I can't live like this. It's torture.

The whole episode had taken less than thirty seconds, but it had felt like thirty minutes. Even as I revelled in those first wonderful breaths, I knew that I would have to go through it all again in an hour or two's time. And that prospect was terrifying.

Sure enough, around sixty minutes later, the same unplug/plug/vacuum/unplug/plug scenario was played out. It was no less painful. I tried to block it out, tried to drift off like I had before, but it was no good. I wanted to say, 'Dear God, please make it stop.' But even with the spell board it would all have been over by the time I'd spelled out the first word.

Having my family around usually made everything seem better, but even Lili's presence couldn't dent my fear of the suction pipe. Or so I thought. It was only when she'd left for the night that I realised the phlegm wouldn't stop forming in my throat just because the day had ended. I would have to be vacuumed throughout the night as well, and now I would have to face it alone. My terror ratcheted up a notch. I couldn't help wondering if night-shift hospital workers were as skilled as their daytime colleagues. Would I even get someone who knew what they were doing?

My meds were turned up, as usual, to induce sleep. I prayed that they would get me through the night. That was probably the ICU medical team's plan as well. But the nightmares came quickly. I dreamed I was being suffocated. Then I opened my eyes and realised it wasn't a dream.

In the event, the nurse doing the suctioning was just as competent as her daytime colleague had been, but being woken by the sensation of my breath suddenly stopping was never going to be an enjoyable experience.

Dealing with the hourly horror of being suctioned in this new way made me forget why I'd been given the trach in the first place. So it came as a surprise when one of Dr Kako's colleagues arrived a couple of days later to put the team's plan into action. The hope was that my diaphragm could be kick-started back into action if I was taken off the ventilator. On the plus side, I already knew the trach pipe could be removed and replaced in a few seconds. The nurses had been doing precisely that at regular intervals over the last two days.

The downside was that I already knew my lungs didn't work when it was out.

So what was the point of the test?

One step ahead of me as usual, the doctor pointed out that it was the balloon-like cuff in my windpipe that stopped me breathing when my trach pipe was removed for suctioning. My diaphragm *might* be working fine. During the lung test, they were planning to deflate the balloon.

'Then we'll see what your lungs are made of.'

In other words, not only was I about to have my air supply switched off, the procedure would take even longer to rectify if nothing happened. How long could I survive without breathing? Did the doctors even know? I was so weak already, how much more could I take? They were gambling on my lungs and diaphragm snapping back into life. If they were wrong, I could be staring death in the face.

I had so many doubts but when the doctor asked if I was ready there was only one answer to give.

Blink.

'Okay,' he said, and gave the rest of the team the instruction to go ahead.

Behind him, a nurse switched off the ventilator. At the same time, another doctor removed the trach pipe from my throat. Then I felt the balloon collapse and my airways clear.

One second. Two seconds. Three. Four.

Come on, come on.

I could tell from the doctor's face that he was willing it to happen almost as much as I was. The only difference was that his life didn't depend on it.

By the time I reached ten I was desperate for the machine to be switched back on. It wasn't working. There was nothing. Nothing but fear.

Eleven. Twelve. Thirteen ...

I stopped counting then and started to lose track of how long I'd been disconnected. In my mind I was scuba diving in Hawaii and the air tank on my back had just run out. I was swimming frantically to reach the surface and my lungs were burning. The flippers were propelling me faster than I'd ever gone before but it wasn't fast enough.

I can't do this. It's too far ...

Another kick.

It's no good. I'm not going to make it.

My whole body was filled with panic. All I wanted was air. They must have seen my eyes darting from left to right. They must have seen my pupils dilating and the hysterical blinking.

Stop. Stop. STOP!

A week earlier, I'd been prepared to go. My mind was set, my path was chosen. I'd even considered fooling the doctors into thinking I was brain-dead to minimise my family's torment. But everything had changed with that wiggle of a toe. Now I wanted to fight. I wanted to be with my wife and daughters.

I didn't want the very people who were charged with helping me to snatch my life away.

The sound of the ventilator kicking back into gear hit me before the first bellow of air. When that finally came I wanted to cry. I'd never known joy like it. How long had I been disconnected? It felt like minutes. But right then it didn't matter. All that mattered was I was alive.

Okay, I needed a machine to breathe, but I was living and thinking. And that was enough for me.

Damn, why didn't we agree on a code beforehand? I need them to know that if my eyes move in a certain way then I'm in trouble. They know my eyes are all I've got. They know that's how I speak. So why don't they watch them when they're doing these things to me?

The breathing experiment hadn't worked, but that didn't stop my medical team proceeding to the next step. After the trauma of the trach pipe, I was loath to give the go-ahead. But wrestling my fear into check, I started to understand that there was a very good reason for everything they were doing, or proposing to do.

They believed in me.

Perhaps it was about time I started believing as well.

Their latest plan was designed to make me stronger and reduce my dependency on the IV stand. In the short term, while I remained in the ICU, it wouldn't make too much difference. But in the mid to long term, it would give me greater mobility. So why didn't I agree to it without a second thought?

Because it involved cutting into my gut.

Ever since I'd arrived at The Queen I'd been fed fluids via the IV drip. But now that I was showing one or two signs that I might live longer than they'd initially predicted, the doctors needed to reverse my weight loss by giving me real food. However, my throat was occupied and my mouth didn't work, so the plan was to pass the food directly into my stomach via a tube. That way I could be fed from a local food source – i.e. a bag resting on my stomach. Then, when the meal was over, they could detach the packet and seal off the connection. That would leave me free to move around without being encumbered by the drip stand. Should I ever regain the use of my limbs, of course.

The theory all sounded reasonable enough. In practice, though, I wasn't so sure. I hadn't realised I hadn't eaten. I couldn't recall feeling hungry. And I'd only felt thirsty because I was so hot. They'd solved that simply by dabbing a wet cloth on my lips. So was this operation really necessary? Did I really want a hose sticking out of my stomach?

On top of that, no one could predict when having tubes connected to my hand might become a problem. I still had zero motion in everything aside from one big toe and my eyes, and, as far as anyone knew, that wasn't about to change. On top of that, if this procedure was as fraught with horror as the diaphragm test had been, then I seriously doubted I wanted to put myself through it.

So my gut instinct was to refuse. But then I considered the

consequences. Would rejecting the procedure keep me strapped to my bed longer than was necessary? Admittedly, there were no guarantees that my condition would improve, but – and it was a huge 'but' – if it did, wouldn't I regret not being in the best position to take advantage of it?

So I agreed.

I'm glad I taught CSI. Without that, half the things they're doing to me would seem straight out of some madman's torture catalogue. I'm still not sure exactly what's going on. More than that, I'm not sure they really know what they're doing, either.

I have to trust them because they're all I have. But, honestly, have they ever seen anything like this before? Have they ever come across someone like me in all of their careers?

The operation, I was informed, was a very minor one. As a result, there was no need to go to theatre. It would take place in the ICU. Then I was simply put to sleep as I had been countless times before.

When I awoke I checked my right hand. One of the drip tubes was missing.

My gown was open at the front. Coiled like a garden hose on my chest were about twelve inches of tubing. I started to look away in horror, but then a sort of morbid fascination drew my eyes back to the tube, and I followed its curls round and round till it snaked its way to a port in my stomach. It was hard for my brain to process at first but eventually I made sense of it. There, on my abdomen, was a thin pipe disappearing into my flesh.

I think the medical team must have tried it out while I was still asleep, because it was another couple of hours before I got to see the tube in action. A nurse arrived with a cheery 'Dinner time', then, once she'd checked that I was okay for her to proceed – blink – she clipped the end of my stomach tube into the aperture of the bag. The liquid inside was beige and thick, like dull custard. I had no idea what it was, but I doubted it was Bird's Instant. It felt heavy and cool on my belly. After about half an hour the bag had drained and the pipe was sealed off again.

Of course, what goes in eventually comes out. Whatever other progress I might have been making, having to use a diaper remained as soul-destroying as it had been on that second day. Despite all the physical problems I had, I just could not accept that other people were wiping my ass. Although I was up for the fight now, prepared to do whatever was necessary to recover, that set me back a little every time.

When I next saw Lili she was as upbeat as ever. Once again I tried to put out of my mind all thoughts of how she must be well practised in remaining cheerful through dealing with her hospice patients. As usual, she limited the conversation to yes/no questions. And, as usual, that was fine by me. If I wanted to say anything in particular I would just flick my eyes to the left, to the little bedside table where the spell board was kept.

Lili wasn't alone in appearing upbeat. The medical team didn't seem fazed by the failure of the diaphragm test, and they'd been buoyed by the success of my new feeding process. I was glad that they were happy, yet I couldn't help thinking that I was probably the first locked-in patient The Queen had ever treated. And certainly the first who had shown any sign of recovery. So were they shooting in the dark? Did they have a plan of action? Or were they making it up as they went along?

By my reckoning, it was now twelve days since I'd been admitted. During that time I'd cheated instant death and had regained the movement in my toe and my eyes. I had one tube to aid my eating and another to aid my breathing. But had the medical team now run out of ideas? I was about to learn that they had not.

Dr Kako walked into the room and informed me that my diaphragm seemed to be on the verge of working again. I looked over to my spell board, so Lili fetched it and started to translate. The only question I spelled out was: 'Why is it so important?'

Dr Kako was ready with the answer. 'When you're no longer dependent on the breathing apparatus you will be able to leave the ICU,' he said. 'You'll be able to enter the second phase of your care.'

The goal of the ICU, he explained, was survival. If I was strong enough to leave, I could start thinking seriously about recovery.

Does he mean that or is he just saying it to convince me to give the go-ahead for another lung test?

On the one hand, I couldn't wait to get better. If leaving the ICU was an important stepping-stone towards that goal, then I should jump to it. But I also had the niggling suspicion – admittedly based only on hearsay – that hospitals, and especially insurance companies, would do anything to hurry patients out of intensive care. I'd been there almost a fortnight, which was verging on the unprecedented. Maybe they just wanted to free up my bed.

If I was going to get out of there, however, I knew I had to put aside any cynicism. So, when Dr Kako announced that they wanted to try turning off the ventilator again, I gave my permission and then promised myself that I would do everything in my power to make it work this time. What exactly I could do to help, I didn't know.

Perhaps I should just force myself not to descend into a dark spiral of panic as soon as I'm unplugged.

Planning to be bold and actually carrying it through are two very different things, though. As soon as I saw the team gathering around me, exactly as they had done earlier in the week, I felt the nerves starting to rise again. I seemed to be producing more spittle, too. Another sign of anxiety.

I tried to concentrate on the outside world to take my mind off what was about to happen. It worked up to a point, but the second I heard the ventilator shutting down I wanted to scream. And when the trach pipe was removed moments later I was overwhelmed by panic again.

Put it back! Put it back!

Where was my spell board when I needed it? I had to let them know I was not happy.

My big toe was restless and my eyes were darting all over the place in a desperate bid to get the staff's attention. But they just ploughed on. What was wrong with Kako? Why couldn't he recognise my distress? Not only were he and the rest of the team apparently oblivious to my pain, they actually seemed to be enjoying themselves.

Come on, guys, this is no smiling matter!

I'd seen movies where patients had to be strapped down in their beds to stop them thrashing around. I knew how they felt. I would have needed a straitjacket to keep me still if I'd had the use of my arms and legs. What they were doing to me was inhumane. It was barbaric. It was . . .

Working.

Everyone was smiling because I was breathing on my own.

CHAPTER FIFTEEN

G. E. T. M. E. O. U. ...

In and out. In and out. In and out. In and out.

I could listen to that sound all day.

The fact that it's coming and going through a hole in my neck is weird. I can't see the hole but I know it's there. I know the tube into my windpipe is somewhere below my chin. I wonder what it looks like, but not enough to ask for a mirror. I just can't envisage how a person can inhale and exhale through a tube. But then, three weeks ago, I couldn't have told you how a person breathes through their mouth.

It's all new to me. New adventures, new fears, new gains. Breathing on my own is the biggest gain yet.

But will it be enough?

I knew I'd taken a major step forwards. But I was also aware I wasn't out of the woods yet. I was still in unknown territory, as were the staff at the Queen of the Valley. They all knew about locked-in syndrome, but I didn't think any of the doctors had treated a patient suffering from it before. And I definitely didn't think they'd come across one who'd learned to breathe again on his own. Given that, what was the next step?

They had to assume I was on the road to recovery. Out of nowhere, I'd regained control of my eyes, my toe, my diaphragm and my lungs. Both the physical extremities of my body and some of my vital organs were back on side. But what did the medical team have in mind for me now? And how far along the road could I reasonably expect to travel?

Whatever the ultimate length of my journey, I was now considered out of immediate critical danger and therefore ready to leave the ICU. In fact, Dr Kako insisted it was time for me to leave the Queen of the Valley altogether. I no longer needed a medical centre. If I were to stand any chance of beating the terrifyingly bleak statistics for locked-in patients, I required therapy, not a recovery facility. Where I went next was a matter for me, Lili and our insurance company.

In between everything else she was doing for me, Lili managed to investigate a multitude of options. I don't know when she found the time to sleep. The day after I started to breathe unaided, she produced an impressive brochure advertising the services of a facility which she thought would be able to help me. The booklet was very professional and the care on offer seemed pretty forward-thinking.

So why was I so angry?

Because this place was a long way from Napa Valley.

After everything I'd been through, this was the first time I'd been furious.

Death's door? I'd handled that.

Complete paralysis? I'd taken that in my stride.

Having my ass cleaned by a stranger? Even that I chalked up as just 'one of those things'.

But this? Moving miles away from home? This would have serious repercussions for other people. I'd already put Lili through so much. She'd been with me every minute she could, and even when she wasn't in the room with me, I knew she'd still be in the building, phoning a friend or speaking to one of the doctors about my care. She'd not had a moment's rest, and that was when she'd been travelling from just up the road. Asking her to make such a long round trip was out of the question for me. Not only was the distance too great but the roads themselves cut through some barren territory and could never be described as highways. What if she had an accident? Or the car broke down? She'd be stranded miles from anywhere and I'd be trussed up like a Thanksgiving turkey unable to do a single thing to help her.

Then there were the kids. Shannon's house – where Melanie was still staying – was forty-five minutes the other side of Napa, so they already had a ninety-minute round trip just to visit me at The Queen. They'd be looking at half a day if I moved to this new facility. Americans are used to driving big distances, but a father couldn't expect his daughters to do that for him.

Besides, Melanie would have to go home some time, Shannon had a job and a family, and Michelle was already back in Alabama. That put an awful lot of pressure on Lili. I prayed she could get through it. I didn't want her to suffer any more than she already had for me.

So, all things considered, I was not happy one bit. And I'm ashamed to say I let Lili know exactly what I thought of her suggestion.

Looking back, if there's anything more ridiculous than an argument via a spell board, then I haven't seen it!

I wanted to save her any more trouble but Lili, being Lili, wouldn't hear any of it. And, knowing she could just put the spell board down at any point, I didn't push my luck. It was barely a day later when I truly wished I had.

But as it turned out, the distance from home was the least of my worries.

And what happens when I get there? I still can't move anything. Dr Kako said I needed physical therapy. What's the point of that when I can't lift a finger?

I don't have a good feeling about this ...

The move went as seamlessly as it could have. Lili was alongside me all the way from the ICU to the ambulance port, with her friend Pat next to her for moral support. Then, when it came to the journey itself, logistically Lili had to travel in her own car. How else would she get home? So I set off in the back of an ambulance knowing that my wife was speeding along somewhere behind us, just as I had two weeks earlier. I knew there was a good reason why she wasn't there, but that didn't stop me wishing she was.

When we slowed down after a while, the paramedic next to me said, 'We're here.'

We stopped, the back doors were yanked open and I felt the sun sweep in. A few minutes later I was riding in its full glare as the gurney was pushed into the building. Nice weather, nice-looking facility and nice people to greet me. It all boded well.

And yet ...

For reasons that will become clear, I've decided not to name the place. Instead I'm going to call it the Facility. Many of the people I met there were very good to me. But unlike the Queen of the Valley, where all the staff, from top to bottom, contributed to a very high level of care, this place had divisions that were not mentioned in the brochure.

I got a bad feeling the second I was admitted. The literature had boasted of a modern, fresh, almost 'designer' interior. But all

I could see from my bed on wheels was a lot of tired décor. My first thought was that the promotional photographs weren't as recent as they might have been.

I was shown – pushed – to my room and was pleasantly surprised to see that I would be sharing it. As much as I had liked my solitude before the stroke, I'd learned that nighttimes alone with just your own thoughts could be taxing. I didn't know what was wrong with the guy who was already in there, but I would soon find out.

The unit was what's called a 'medium-care facility'. That is to say it is the next rung down the ladder from intensive care. Patients are not in any imminent danger of death, which was great for me to hear after the prognosis I'd been given just two weeks earlier. People went there to recuperate and build up their strength, however long that took. As I looked around the room, I hoped it wouldn't take too long. There was a curtain dividing the space in half, and my side wasn't big enough for much more than the bed and a galley on one side for the nurses and visitors to congregate. But far worse than the cramped conditions was the sound coming from the other side of the curtain.

I think it's Spanish, I thought, as I listened to the anxious prayers of clearly a very nervous man. For the next hour, he didn't stop speaking, babbling away in a Latin tongue, calling on his deity to do something for him. As soon as I realised the guy wasn't going to stop, I managed to tune him out. I had my own problems to worry about.

The doctor who came to see me a little later sounded very excited to be working with a locked-in patient. I was the first he'd seen, he said. He ordered his staff to get me bedded in as quickly and comfortably as possible. My catheter had to be hooked up, the suction machine that would be fed into my trach hole every few hours was wheeled in and tested, and my feed bags were readied for connection to my stomach tube. There was a feeling of against-the-clock action, but I couldn't complain about the level of care. And I had Lili to thank for that.

Yet again, I don't know where she found the time, but after everything had been organised she produced a laminated, ring-bound 'book' of about four pages. On each page were several large-print questions. She showed it to the doctor and the nurses who would be taking care of me.

'If you see Rich looking at this book, then please pick it up and ask him the questions, one by one, until you get to what it is he needs.'

She ran through a few sample questions.

'Do you need suctioning?'

I'd blink yes or no.

'Do you need to be changed?'

One blink or two.

'Are you too hot?'

One blink meant bring me the fan.

It was such a simple idea but it saved us all a lot of time and me a lot of discomfort. The staff were particularly grateful. Anything to make their job more efficient was to be commended. In fact, even before Lili had left for the day, one of the nurses established – via the book – that I did indeed need a fresh diaper. Lili, by then, had been absent for an hour filling in forms and paperwork on my behalf in the office area.

Because of the distance she had to travel, it was only six o'clock when Lili started saying goodbye. I was sad to see her go, obviously, but relieved she'd be driving home in daylight. That was the more important consideration. She promised to be back by ten the following morning. I started the countdown right then.

For the rest of the evening I mainly listened to the guy on the other side of the curtain. He hadn't stopped praying since the moment I'd arrived. I learned that he'd been diagnosed with acute kidney failure and wasn't expected to leave there alive. The constant appeals to God were his way of pleading for a stay of execution.

Paradoxically, something about his panic gave me strength. I'd been where he was; I'd almost tasted the other side of the divide. But I'd managed to crawl back up to something approaching safety. I had no idea how long that would last. For now, though, I was content to keep fighting.

The day staff disappeared at some point and the evening doctor was quick to introduce himself. My suctioning was done competently, my catheter bag was emptied, my food was introduced at the appropriate time and then two guys came in and told me they were going to turn me. This had to happen every four or five hours. Without constant movement, I was in danger of developing bedsores or, worse, deep-vein thrombosis, caused by staying in one position for too long. On top of everything else, another blood clot could quite easily kill me.

After such a proficient start I had no reason to believe my care would be any different than it had been at the Queen of the Valley. But being so far from Lili was still playing on my mind. In fact, I was thinking about it so intently that it was a couple of hours before I realised a member of staff hadn't attended to me since the two guys had left. And I only noticed it then because I started to feel the familiar build-up of mucus in my throat.

I need suctioning. How long has it been since my last one?

The guy on the other side of the curtain had finally stopped ranting, so I figured it was probably after midnight. I assumed another shift change was taking place, which would keep everyone busy for a few minutes, but then it would be back to business as usual as soon as everyone had settled into their roles.

Ten or so minutes later, there was still no sign of any doctors or nurses, and the build-up of phlegm in my throat was getting serious. I hadn't felt like this since my first day in the ICU. What the hell was going on? Where was everyone?

Finally the door opened. *Thank God.* But no one came in. A head just poked around the frame, took one look at me, then disappeared again.

Is that it? Is that my hourly check-up?

I might have been okay with it if I thought the night staff were rushed off their feet. But all I could hear coming from the corridors was loud talking and laughter.

It must have been about one o'clock before I saw another human being. I really should have been asleep by then but I was too scared to close my eyes. I was afraid I might choke to death.

This time the nurse came in and looked me over as she would a patient in a coma. But of course I was fully awake. I felt as if I were a piece of meat on a butcher's block. Frantically, I started looking at the 'book'. I was desperate for her to pick it up and go through my questions. That was the quickest way to tell her I needed suctioning.

But she never looked at my eyes.

What's she playing at? She knows that's the only way I can communicate.

Then another – even more terrifying – thought occurred to me:

Or maybe she doesn't she know anything of the sort.

She was certainly behaving as if she didn't understand there was anyone fully conscious inside this useless hunk of a body.

She'd probably seen dozens of coma victims during her career, and, as far as she was concerned, I was just another one of them. I had to face facts. Either she'd been told I had locked-in syndrome and had chosen to ignore it, or no one had bothered to explain the difference between my condition and a coma.

It was another hour before she returned. This time she did pick up the book. She began to read out the first question in an accent not dissimilar to that of the guy on the other side of the curtain. Then she did the same with the second. But she never looked over to see if I was blinking in response. About halfway through the third question she tutted, sighed, then tidied the book away somewhere behind my head. Next she pondered my spell board for a few seconds before putting it in the same place. Now I couldn't even point to either of my communication devices with my eyes.

It's like she doesn't even understand what they're for.

As I listened to the noise continuing outside, I realised that everyone was shouting and joking in Spanish. If English wasn't their first language, were they going to understand my condition?

I wondered whether 'locked-in' even translated into Spanish. Was that why the nurse was ignoring me? It reminded me of my first couple of days at the ICU, when no one had spoken to me. Almost all of them had just got on with their business without interacting with me in any way. But in this place it was worse. They must have thought I was already gone.

Then, though, it dawned on me that the nurses never bothered attending to my roommate, either, not even when he awoke and started calling out in terror. I began to wonder whether they were trained nurses at all.

Despite my desire to stay awake I must have drifted off at some point through exhaustion, because I awoke to find I had a soiled diaper. But that was nothing compared with the real problem.

I was in serious danger of drowning now.

It gave me no comfort to know that I'd gone through the same ordeal several times already and had always survived. In fact, it was more terrifying than ever because I'd lost all faith in the medical staff.

I don't think I'm going to make it through the night ...

By now, the build-up of phlegm was becoming critical. I tried to stay calm but it was impossible. It's one thing to prepare for death when you think the doctors are about to switch off your machines. I was able to deal with that because I knew it would be quick and relatively painless. By contrast, I couldn't imagine anything worse than slow suffocation. But now I didn't have to imagine it, because it was happening to me. And all the time, all I could think was:

I'm going to die tonight and I haven't even said goodbye to Lili.

I'm not sure how I got here. I'm in a McDonald's, waiting in line to be served. A bright-faced Hispanic girl cheerfully takes my order. She understands me perfectly until I try to ask her a question. Her English doesn't stretch that far. I look to her colleagues for help. They're all laughing and partying at the back, not serving anyone. And now my own helper is laughing so much she forgets all about me.

I wake up and see the face from the dream peering around the door. She doesn't come in.

When my eyes flicked open in the morning, I honestly couldn't believe I was still alive.

Surely there was no way I could have survived the night?

It seemed that I had, though, because a nurse was standing

next to me, seconds away from suctioning the mucus from my windpipe, judging by the equipment in her hand. I couldn't believe it. Why had she decided to do it now, all of a sudden?

'You've got a lot of secretions today,' she said, and immediately I realised the staff must have changed over. 'I'll make a note about that for the doctor.'

I searched frantically for my spell board. If I could make her pick it up, I would spell out that I hadn't been suctioned all night. But I couldn't see it anywhere. Then I remembered. The night nurse had put it behind my head – the one place I couldn't indicate with my eyes. Something else to add to my complaints sheet – if I ever got the chance.

The new nurse was friendly enough and a breath of fresh air after the nightmare shift she'd replaced. Then a doctor came in shortly afterwards and ran through his daily checks. It must have been at least another hour before the door opened again and Lili marched in. She was smiling but seemed flustered. Whatever reassurances she'd offered about the long journey, it was obviously already taking its toll.

She started talking the second she entered the room. I liked that about her. It was just news about which friends had sent their love, people who'd got in touch and people she was going to tell about this or that, but it was such a comfort to hear her voice. By the time she'd taken off her coat, leaned over to kiss me and sat down, I could see she was looking for something.

'Where's the book?'

I tried to achieve the impossible and look behind my own head. Lili was understandably confused, so she stood up and started scanning the room for the book herself. It didn't take her long to find it. She started running through the questions and I blinked twice in response to each one as quickly as I could. As soon as she'd finished, I rolled my eyes towards the spell board, which Lili had placed on the table next to me when she'd recovered the book.

'You want to say something, honey?'

Blink.

'Okay, let me grab the pen.'

The spell board had revolutionised my life, but it was so laborious to use that I never wasted time on pleasantries. Lili didn't expect me to, either. By the same token, she didn't expect me to be quite as blunt as I was now.

G. E. T. M. E. O. U. T. O. F. H. E. R. E.

She looked nonplussed. 'Did something happen last night?'

The real answer was 'No, *nothing* happened – that's the point', but it was easier to blink once for yes.

Lili switched from concerned wife into medical professional.

'Was there a problem with your care?'

Blink.

She looked down at the spell board and, I imagined, remembered finding it out of my view.

'Did the night shift use the book?'

Blink. Blink.

'Did they change and turn you?'

Blink. Blink.

'Did they feed you?'

Blink. Blink.

'Oh my God. Tell me they at least suctioned your trach pipe?'

Blink. Blink.

She knew I must be tired from the message I'd just spelled out, but she needed to know more. So, over the next twenty minutes, I told her as much as I could, one letter at a time. By the end of it, she knew for sure I wasn't complaining just because I didn't like being so far from Napa. My life had been placed in jeopardy. I'd managed to spell that out.

'Okay, honey, leave it to me.' Then, as she rose from her seat: 'I'm so sorry for bringing you here.'

She had left before I could tell her it wasn't her fault. On paper, it had seemed a perfect fit for my needs, if a little out of the way. The day staff and the evening team had been great. It was just the night shift who had let me down.

I didn't know where she intended to go or who she intended to see. What I did know was that she would be tearing the place apart to get some answers. When she came back about half an hour later, she had a face like thunder. The second she saw me, the professional face returned, but I'd already seen her true mood.

'They're going to do what they can to improve things here,' she said. 'And I'm going to try to get you transferred. I just hope people are working today.'

It was a Friday. She didn't have to add, 'Because I won't have any chance over the weekend.'

Lili left early to make the arrangements. Luckily, I then had a couple of other visitors. They stayed with me during the afternoon shift change. My level of care remained high, but these weren't the workers who terrified me.

I tried my best to fall asleep before the midnight changeover. It would be safer for me that way, I figured. At least I wouldn't be able to work myself up into a panic. But with the naps throughout the day and the prayers from the other side of the curtain as loud as ever, drifting off proved impossible. It must have been one in the morning before I even felt drowsy. And by then I hadn't had a single visit from the night team.

Nothing has changed.

It was just as bad as the previous night. No one came in, no one did anything, no one seemed to care. By two o'clock I was seriously panicking again. I might have survived the previous night, but that was no guarantee I'd make it through this one. I could hear my mucus bubbling. I'd been lucky once. Was my good fortune about to run out?

Two o'clock turned into three. As I listened to the gurgling in my throat I felt like the condemned man hearing the hangman's footsteps approach. Closer and closer, louder and louder. It was surely only a matter of time before the footsteps stopped and everything went black.

This is not right. This not right. This is not …

I don't know whether I fell asleep or blacked out, whether I slipped into unconsciousness through panic or exhaustion.

In the morning, as I came round, Lili couldn't tell me. She was already sitting next to me when I opened my eyes. My windpipe was clear. The mucus had been vacuumed out. When had that happened? Had I managed to sleep through a suctioning? I must have been tired.

The horrors of the night were still fresh in my mind, but the first few minutes after waking brought even more vivid flashbacks. I think Lili noticed. I almost felt guilty telling her about my ordeal, knowing she would take it personally. I was right. As she put the spell board down, she was numb with rage.

Why hadn't anyone listened to her complaints? This wasn't just criticism of the décor. Her husband's life was under threat because of inadequate care.

For a few seconds I saw my own emotions mirrored in Lili's face. We were both impotent and ignored. Irrelevant and in the way. I prayed it would be the closest she ever came to experiencing the frustrations I felt every second I was awake.

Suddenly, though, her expression cleared and she snapped

into action. Professional Lili was taking control. As she marched out of the room I almost felt pity for whoever was about to experience her fury.

When she returned ten minutes later she was no less angry. A whole new set of staff was on for the weekend. What's more, the administrators at the other facilities all worked Monday to Friday. So I was stuck in this place for at least another two nights. I'd never seen Lili so deflated. She seemed to think she'd failed me in some way. But in reality she was the only one trying to fix the problem.

Lili may have drawn a blank getting me out of the building, but she did manage to get me out of my room.

'It's not much,' she said, 'but at least you won't be kept awake by you-know-who any more.'

As it turned out, there was another advantage to shifting rooms.

'Pleased to meet you, Rich,' the guy in the next bed called out as I was wheeled in. 'My name is Franks.'

Almost anyone would have been an improvement on the nightmare roommate I'd just left behind, but 'Mr Franks', as Lili and I called him, proved to be a far better companion than I ever could have expected. He was a young guy who'd lost a lot of weight and was being treated for the bedsores he'd accumulated over a lifetime of being crushed by his own body. But he had a mischievous sense of humour that I could relate to and he would not stand for slack service from anyone. During the day he kept me amused, but he really came into his own at night. When he saved my life.

I thought I was the only person who could hear the mucus building up in my throat, but it turned out that Mr Franks could hear it too.

'Hey, we need some attention in here,' he called out. 'My friend Rich needs his suctioning.'

Ten minutes later, a trio of nervous-looking nurse aides were standing around me, trying to figure out how to work the suction machine. Mr Franks didn't take his eyes off them for a second. He'd seen the process several times during the evening and noticed as soon as they went off track. At which point he let them know all about it.

The vacuuming was even more painful than usual, but it was far better than the alternative. I only wished I could have shaken Mr Franks's hand and thanked him.

He probably didn't even know he'd just saved a drowning man.

CHAPTER SIXTEEN

We're Going to Send You for a Few Tests

Apricots.

 Apricots and cherries. I can picture them now. Filling my garden with colour. They should be ripe now, too.

 I wonder if Lili could pick a few for me.

 Don't be stupid. As if she doesn't have enough to do.

 I wonder if she's even been out in the garden. Is it still daylight when she gets home?

 What else will need doing? The fava beans should be ready any time. And the lettuce. And the rhubarb.

 But there's nothing I can do about it. What a shame.

 I guess the fruit flies are going to have a feast this year.

I survived the weekend, with Mr Franks's help.

 The good news was that Lili managed to find a new medium-care facility for me. The bad news was that it wouldn't have a space until the end of the week. In the meantime, I would just have to make it through the nights as best I could.

 At least my care during daylight hours was still generally good,

although even that had hiccups. Things got off to a bad start on
Monday when the guys who came in to rotate me were a little exu-
berant. One of them had done it several times already, but I'd never
seen the other one before. Unfortunately, the experienced one took
my feet, which meant the new boy was left with my head. I don't
think he'd ever lifted anyone in his life. He just grabbed my shoulders and, when his pal said 'go', rolled me over onto my side. What
he didn't do was support my head in any way. I still had zero control over my neck, so my skull just slammed down onto the pillow.

The pain was excruciating. I had never wanted to cry out as
much as I did then. You wouldn't move a baby without supporting
its head – so why had they just rolled me over like that? I may have
looked like a statue, but I wasn't made of stone. My joints and muscles were as flexible as anyone else's.

There was such a snap as my head fell that I was amazed no
one else heard it. If I hadn't been paralysed from the neck down
already, I was pretty sure I was now. Even with the jabbing pain
still pulsing through me, I knew I had to try the only test at my dis-
posal to establish if I had been critically injured. It took a lot of
concentration, but eventually I managed to move the big toe on
my left foot. I could feel it rubbing against the sheet. So at least my
neck wasn't broken. But it must have been a close-run thing.

On a brighter note, when I was returned to my customary
position on my back a few hours later – more carefully this time –
a new comfort aid was brought in for me.

'We need to give some thought to your circulation,' my doctor
said. 'Being still so long can cause problems there.'

His solution was to elevate my arms on pillows so the blood
flow would be more dynamic. Similar cushions were placed under
my feet, too.

I could understand the science, so I was happy to go along

with it. And I was even happier that this doctor really seemed to care about my rehabilitation.

He genuinely thinks I'm going to get a bit better if we do this.

However, while this daylight-hours doctor was doing everything in his power to improve my quality of life, the nocturnal shift seemed to me to be hell bent on making it as uncomfortable as possible.

Bearing in mind I literally couldn't lift a finger, I don't know how my arm slipped off the raised pillow during the night. But I woke up to find it wedged down the side of the bed, between the mattress and the steel bars. It hurt so much I couldn't even pinpoint at first what was wrong. In addition to being crushed by the metal and the mattress, the arm was twisted at both shoulder and elbow. It felt like it was in the jaws of a snarling dog and there was nothing I could do about it. Mr Franks was sound asleep, so I stayed like that throughout the night. Even when I had my windpipe suctioned, the nurse aides didn't touch my arm. I guess they thought someone senior to them actually wanted me lying in that position and they weren't going to use any initiative to question that. It was only when the two guys came to move me in the morning that I got any relief.

Even though he must have known that Lili and I couldn't wait to get out of there, the doctor in charge of my day care pressed on diligently with my rehab. Part of his plan was to implement a regime of physical exercise. Even though I couldn't move a muscle aside from one toe and my eyes, he told me that therapists would be coming in to lift my limbs and put them through the motions. The idea was that this would remind my muscle memory what it felt like to move.

On my first scheduled appointment, however, the therapist had barely touched my leg when he stopped.

'I need to check something with the doctor,' he said, then ran out.

A few minutes later, my calf was being kneaded by a group of medics. According to them, it felt unusually hard.

'It's probably nothing to worry about, but we're going to send you for a few tests,' the doctor said.

Within an hour, I was in an ambulance heading to Marin General Hospital. Once there, I was put through a CAT scanner again. Lili took her familiar place in the control booth, away from the radiation. Afterwards I was told the results.

'I'm afraid you have a small blood clot in your leg,' the doctor explained. 'I'm going to give you a blood-thinning agent called Coumadin, which should disperse it. I'm also going to prescribe a course of Fragmin, which is an anticoagulant. That, in turn, should stop you forming any more clots. I'm confident that with these measures you will make a full recovery. However, in the meantime, we will have to put your exercise programme on hold.'

I'd become agitated at the very mention of the word 'clot'.

Could this cause another stroke?

There was no need for the spell board. Lili asked the question for me.

'In theory, yes, if the clot moves and blocks the blood supply to your brain or reaches your heart or lungs. But that is highly unlikely, and I'm pretty sure the thinning agent will work.'

He sounded incredibly confident. So why wasn't I?

Because if he was wrong, I knew that another clot, however small, would end my life in an instant.

Is this my life now? Two clots in three weeks. Are they related? Have I done something to bring them on? Is it hereditary?

Oh my God, have I passed this on to my kids?

It doesn't square with what I know about blood clots. But then I can't even work out why I had one in the first place. Me having two is like a bad joke.

I wonder how they were able to find the second one so quickly. Is the one in my leg a remnant of the one in my neck? Have they been monitoring it? Or does my leg really feel much tougher with the clot inside?

If they can spot a minor clot in my leg, why couldn't I spot a major one in my neck? What am I always telling my students? 'Work the clues.' Was there a sign I missed?

I rack my brains. Could I have avoided all this? Did I really have to put my family through this hell?

Just the idea that I'm somehow responsible is enough to make me cry – if only I could do that.

I arrived back at the Facility even more morose than when I'd left. Not only was I facing the prospect of another three days – or rather nights – of torture: I'd now be making no progress during the days, either. With rehab out of the question, what was there for my doctors to do with me.

They'll have to work hard to earn their money now . . .

The next day, when one of the therapists came in to see me he brought a small, flat gadget that looked like an alarm button you'd find on a wall. And that, pretty much, was what it was.

'We're going to put this to the side of your head,' he explained. 'If you need someone at any time of the day – or, more importantly, I think, at night – you just need to roll your head to the right and you will activate the trigger. Any movement at all will throw the switch, so you barely need to touch it. Do you think you can do that?'

In a word? *No!*

Of course I couldn't do it. I was locked rigid onto the bed. The only time I ever moved was when two burly men rolled me over. And even that had left me with severe pain in my neck. In much the same way as the therapist's laughable idea had.

The therapist wasn't swayed, though. He planted the little box against the side of my head as closely as he could. Another millimetre and its corner would have dug into my temple.

It makes no difference how near you place it. I'm never going to be able to move, let alone hit a target.

None the less, after a few minutes, I started trying. At least that took my mind off the tedium of the day and the horrors of the night to come. In fact, I continued to try all night. By the next morning I was still struggling, intermittently, even while Lili and my other visitors were sitting alongside me. They wouldn't have known. As usual, nothing moved aside from my eyes.

But when they'd left for the evening something strange happened.

Was that a twitch?

I could swear I felt something. Had my pillow moved?

No! I honestly think it was me.

I tried again. Just as I'd once channelled everything I had into wiggling my toe, I now focused everything I had onto my neck. Overcoming the pain was the hardest part, but once I'd managed to block that out I was able to concentrate on moving it.

Time stood still for a few seconds, maybe a few minutes. I really felt like I was getting somewhere. I thought about the alarm on my pillow. I thought about how I just needed to turn my head a few degrees to reach it.

Come on, come on.

Then it happened. My neck gave a little spasm and my head swung to the right. One degree, two, three, four, six, eight, ten –

and it didn't stop there. It probably turned about fifteen degrees before my temple hit something. Hard.

The alarm!

I'd moved so far and so suddenly that I'd knocked the gadget clean off the pillow and onto the floor. I couldn't believe it. I'd managed to move my head, but the very thing I needed to tell someone all about it had been sent flying.

After that, the night didn't seem anything like as bad as the others. I still relied on Mr Franks to holler out whenever I needed the nurse aides to come and vacuum away my phlegm, but just knowing that I'd regained some movement in my neck, the very place where the clot had nearly killed me, was a massive morale boost. I wondered whether the original clot buster had finally worked its magic. Or perhaps the Coumadin was responsible.

Either way, I couldn't wait to tell Lili. I couldn't wait to tell my doctors. Most of all, I couldn't wait to get on with the rest of my rehab. For the first time in three weeks, I began to see a flicker of light at the end of the tunnel.

And this time I was pretty sure it wasn't attached to the front of a train …

CHAPTER SEVENTEEN

Where Would You Like to Go?

I should be doing crunches now.

It's morning, I'm being prepared to be wheeled to an ambulance, and I'm thinking about my old routine while I wait. Crunches, bench presses, dead lifts, squats, upright rows, biceps curls. When did I last do any of them? Let me think. It's 11 June now. I was admitted to the Queen of the Valley on 20 May. So that's three weeks without a workout.

I used to miss the burn if I skipped a single day. My body's going to kill me the next time I step inside a gym.

Wait a minute, who am I kidding? All I've managed to do since 20 May is wiggle my toe and turn my head half an inch. When am I ever going to be in a locker room again? When am I ever going to be smelling liniment or Deep Heat?

I feel like I could cry again.

Do I give in to it? Do I accept I'm never going to lift a weight again? Or do I fight?

As the orderlies surround me to start pushing me out to the waiting ambulance, I know which path I want to take. But what's the point? It doesn't matter what my mind wants, does it?

It's all up to my body now.

After eight days and seven horrendous nights at the Facility, Lili finally managed to get me transferred to the Care Meridian facility in Fairfax, Marin County. Obviously, that was a huge relief, but I was also disappointed I wasn't heading back to Napa. Fairfax is actually even further from home, so I really didn't want to go there. Once again, I'm ashamed to say I resented Lili for choosing the place. And my mood didn't improve as soon as I saw what lay beyond the ambulance doors. Whereas the Facility had been in a peaceful setting, now I was being unloaded alongside the four-lane Sir Francis Drake Boulevard. But then the Facility had turned out to be nine layers of hell for me, so I knew that appearances could be deceptive.

Maybe I should give this place a chance.

The facility looked like a one-storey house from the outside, and the homely theme continued inside. The corridors felt like hallways, walking – or being wheeled – into the reception was like entering somebody's lounge, and my room had the appearance of a proper bedroom, not a science lab. Yes, there were plenty of plugs and sockets, and machines in the corner, but the wardrobe and dresser were wooden rather than flat-pack plastic. Little things like that made a difference.

Another homely touch was the absence of a curtain separating me from my new roommate. I also noticed that light from the windows was able to reach every corner of the room, so the ambience was definitely an improvement on what I'd been used to. But then a thought struck me:

This could go either way. It all depends on who I'm sharing with.

I needn't have worried. Watching my arrival with quiet interest was a cheery guy called John. He couldn't have been nicer, chatting away about what a great choice I'd made. I didn't see Lili roll her eyes at me when she heard that, but I wouldn't have blamed her if she did. I knew that no one could have tried harder to find me a place in Napa, so it was wrong to blame her for getting me transferred here, especially as Care Meridian seemed, on the face of it, perfect for my needs. It had only a dozen patients, compared with the Facility's industrial-scale 360; and each nurse attended to just one patient, not nine. Also everything was on one floor, which made wheelchair access easier. I hoped that might soon be an important feature for me.

So the early signs were very good. Still, they'd initially been good at the Facility, too.

Care Meridian is set up to rehabilitate patients into the community, at whatever level they can achieve. The focus is less on medical treatment than on getting mind and body prepared for release back into the outside world. For me, that process would involve three different types of therapy session per day, the doctor explained. Looking at his watch, he said, 'We're only going to have time for one today, but I think you'll enjoy it.'

As if on cue, a smiling, dark-haired man in a blue smock entered the room.

'Hello, Richard. My name's Dennis. I'm your physical therapist.' Then, even before the doctor had left the room, he added, 'Shall we get to work?'

Dennis must have been in his sixties but he had the physique of a man half his age. I soon learned he also had a deep aversion to the word 'can't' that bordered on the psychotic. As he ran through his plans for me, occasionally he would pause and say, 'If you're thinking, "I can't do that," then stop right now because I'm here to tell you that you can.' He was just about the most positive person I'd ever met in my life. I was glad to have him on my side – even if I didn't share his optimism.

Sharing a room with John really brought home to me what

the future might hold. He was a paraplegic. He couldn't move below his waist and the prognosis was that he never would. What was so different about me? Who was to say that I would ever regain any more strength than he would? I needed to be realistic. I would settle for getting out of hospital and being as light a burden on Lili and my daughters as possible. Right there, right then, that seemed the best I could hope for. From what I could tell behind the doctors' inscrutable faces, their aspirations were in the same ballpark. Only Dennis seemed not to have read the brief.

He couldn't touch my left leg because apparently the DVT was still present. He hoped it would be clear in a week or so. But in the meantime there was plenty he could do with my other leg and my two arms. He picked up my right arm, surprisingly gently for such a big man, and, describing everything as he went along, began to manipulate my elbow in a range of exercises. First he lifted my wrist up to my head, while supporting the joint; then he raised the arm right above my head and rotated it in a circular motion. For all his gentleness, it was weirdly tiring considering I wasn't putting in any effort myself.

He worked on the three limbs like that for an hour, coaxing little movements out of my joints. If he didn't, he said, they would seize up and my muscles would atrophy. I didn't know how much weight I'd lost since I'd first been admitted to The Queen, but I could tell from my emaciated raised arms and leg that my muscle definition had significantly diminished. What had taken years to build up had disappeared in a matter of weeks.

For all Dennis's upbeat running commentary, I couldn't help feeling like a spectator, rather than a participant, in all the exercises. I could see it was my leg that was bending, but I still had no control over it, so it may as well have belonged to John in the next bed. Nevertheless, at the end of the session, Dennis congratulated me on my 'work'. We both knew that I hadn't done anything at all, but that was his style. He wanted me to share his positive mental attitude and assured me I'd be amazed by what that could achieve.

His enthusiasm for his work was infectious, and he certainly did give me a new feeling of optimism. Up to that point, my greatest ambition had been to beat the various forecasts – life expectancy, degree of mobility and so on – for the average locked-in sufferer. On my best days at the Facility, I had started to believe I might achieve that. And now, with Dennis to help me, I was almost convinced of it.

But he expected more. He wanted my body back, operational and fully under my control. I had to admire his spirit, but right there and then, with my tired and still useless arms lying by my sides, I could not think of anything less likely.

I'm watching my wrist rise towards my shoulder. The elbow doesn't move. Perfect technique for a biceps curl, but those days are gone. I need to accept that now. I'm not even doing the lifting.

Dennis is a good guy. His heart's in the right place. But I've had people wiping my ass for a month. I'm not going to be lifting so much as a toilet seat any time soon. If ever.

There's no point getting my hopes up. Whatever he says.

After a few hours of feeling sorry for myself, I started to reassess my situation. My ambition in the ICU had been merely to survive the stroke. Later, it was just to survive the Facility. But now actual recovery was being presented to me as a viable possibility.

Apart from the cheerleading ebullience of Dennis, there was another very strong motivation to respond to my treatment. Care Meridian was a sophisticated rehabilitation facility and as such, I imagined, it must have been expensive. According to the terms of my healthcare insurance, the doctors had to be confident I was either making progress or about to. If I showed no – or too few – signs of improvement then the funding for my treatment would be cut and I'd be moved to a nursing home or even a hospice. In other words, the medical world would give up on me and I would merely be nursed towards death. In the US, there's no NHS to scoop up the underprivileged. If you can't pay for your treatment, you're denied access to it.

At that moment, I knew the doctors were still exploring my chances. It was the therapy team, and Dennis in particular, who saw my potential. So, regardless of my scepticism, I swore to myself that I would cooperate to the best of my ability and make the most of my stay, however long that may prove to be.

But that wasn't going to be easy, especially as my other 'life support' wouldn't be there so much from now on.

I don't know how Lili had managed it up to that point, but having her around every day had undoubtedly helped save my life. Without the promise of seeing her face every morning in the ICU and especially at the Facility, I'm not sure I would even have wanted to wake up. But in the real world she had a job – a very important one – and she needed to get back to it. She had negotiated different hours, so she would still be able to visit me several days a week. But given the distance, it wasn't practical – or, in my opinion, safe – for her to come any more frequently. Fortunately, Melanie would be coming by most days anyway, as would Shannon whenever she could get away from her job. On top of that, I was looking forward to visits from my sister Carol, and plenty of good Napa friends, like David and Colleen and Keith and Pam, had also promised to make the trip at weekends. All things considered, I felt blessed.

Meanwhile, my new environment really was very comfortable.

The staff were uniformly considerate, skilled and capable. They were also not afraid to learn. Of the six or so people I met on my first day, not one had seen a spell board before, which should not have been too surprising since none of them had ever met a locked-in sufferer, either. But with Lili's help I was able to demonstrate how to use it. In conjunction with Lili's book, I was then able to communicate with everyone who was overseeing my healthcare. It was a significant advance after the Facility because I now felt I was being treated like a fully conscious human being again.

That was important to me. Fortunately, it was high on Care Meridian's agenda as well, and that started with the staff, in particular the ones who would be taking care of my daily needs. Arthur and Margarita were my two daytime carers, then Brenda would take over for the evening shift. Arthur was a Filipino guy of about thirty and I knew we would get on the first time we met. He hadn't been in the room long when he noticed my diaper needed changing. As mortifying as it always was to rely on someone else to do that for me, the fact that it was pretty much Arthur's introduction to me left me feeling even more humiliated than usual. As a way of breaking the ice, it quite literally stank.

At least it can't get any worse, I suppose.

Or so I thought, until Arthur was leaning over to wipe me clean – and I farted.

Luckily, he just laughed it off. 'Well, Rich, you could have warned me!'

I think that put us both at ease, and from then on I felt entirely comfortable with him.

It wasn't long before I met the other member of my daycare team. Margarita was a tiny Mexican woman but even though she was barely five foot tall, she was as strong as an ox – a fact she proved shortly after entering the room.

'Bath time,' she announced in her thick accent, a smile playing on her lips.

I wished that I had a blinking sequence for 'Excuse me?' Maybe I could work something out with Lili in the morning.

As if reading my mind, Margarita said, 'You don't think being in a bed is going to get you out of bathing, do you?' and laughed. I knew then I hadn't misheard. What I didn't know, though, was how she intended to get me into a tub. I may have lost weight, but I was still convinced that this was mission impossible.

Nevertheless, once Arthur had wheeled the gurney over, Margarita took down the bars from the side of my bed and then flipped me effortlessly onto the trolley. I heard John chuckling from the bed across the room. Clearly he knew what was coming next.

I was still getting over the surprise of Margarita's superhuman strength when we arrived at what looked like a fully equipped bathroom – but with a difference. To the sound of running water, she unbuttoned my gown and for the first time in weeks I saw how emaciated my body had become. I was used to the trach pipe in my throat, the catheter in my penis with its urine bag to the side, and the feeding tube in my stomach, but this was something new and deeply shocking.

The running water was filling a giant whirlpool bath. I wondered why they needed such a big tub but I soon found out. First the nurses manoeuvred my naked frame onto what I thought was a plastic table top alongside the bath. Then, at the press of a button, the table top transformed into something much more impressive, gliding sideways until it was suspended over the whirlpool. Finally, it began to descend until the whole platform – and my body, up to just below my trach pipe – was submerged in the foaming water.

I had not felt anything so good in weeks. The warm water on my skin was therapy in itself. Then when the power jets were turned on I got a massage and a bubble bath in one. Margarita also shampooed my hair and scrubbed every part of me clean. It was a better bath than I'd ever had at home.

Buoyed by all the care and attention, I returned to my room thinking that Brenda, the evening carer, had a lot to live up to. But she managed it. She was a sweetheart, working meticulously to position a call button on my pillow in exactly the right spot so I could press it without fear of its tumbling out of the bed again. She was also happy to chat away long after her checks were done, filling the void left by the empty guest chairs. Without my having to say a word, she could sense how affected I was when my visitors left that evening. Before she left herself, she asked which TV channel I wanted. Then she dispensed the medicine to help me sleep and wished me sweet dreams.

I couldn't have been in better spirits and I was determined to get through my first night without any of the nightmares that had plagued my stay at the Facility. Listening to the staff outside my room talking to each other in English – which meant I could understand them and they could also understand me and my notes – went a long way to helping with that, and I drifted off peacefully. I was even grateful when I was woken up, which happened at regular intervals, because that meant they were conscientiously checking if my windpipe needed suctioning. Aside from those vacuuming sessions, I slept like a baby for the first time in over a week.

The following morning I embarked on what would become my schedule for as long as I remained at Care Meridian. Whether that would be ten weeks or ten years, I felt, was up to me. I didn't want to dwell on the consequences of its being a decade, so I concentrated on what was happening right then.

The day began, once the changeover of staff was complete, with a thorough bed bath from Margarita. (She promised I'd have the full whirlpool experience again the following day.) Then she combed my hair, cleaned my teeth, shaved me with an electric razor and changed my diaper – even though it was unsoiled. Such attention to detail really impressed me.

My doctor came to visit around eight o'clock. He seemed happy enough with my condition but said he wanted to check I'd had no repercussions from the physical therapy. Not only was I fine, but the DVT had virtually disappeared, so I'd soon be able to work on both legs.

Before then, however, I had to get used to another form of treatment. If I'd thought Dennis was underestimating the challenge ahead of him, I felt my next therapist, Kahlin, had a mountain to climb. I didn't envy her job at all. In fact, from the moment she introduced herself as my speech therapist, I wished she would just go for a nice long walk. At least then both of us wouldn't be wasting our time.

Ignoring my cynicism, Kahlin went through the various techniques she was going to employ and explained the results she was hoping to see. I listened politely at first, but when she mentioned that it was also her job to get me eating again, I started tuning her out. The woman was deluded. I had zero control over my jaw and tongue, and I had a hole and a tube in my throat, for God's sake. Given all that, how was I meant to speak or eat?

Poor Kahlin. At least Dennis could move my arms and legs manually. She could hardly grab my tongue and vocal cords and try to coax them back into life.

Boy, this is going to be a long hour ...

At some point in the morning Melanie arrived. Finally, I thought, an injection of sanity in the room. At least she wouldn't expect me to jump through impossibly high hoops. And yet, when my next session began, she became quite the cheerleader.

Christine introduced herself as my occupational therapist. I needed that one explained. After all, I already had an occupation. Or at least I used to have one. I'd been absent so long perhaps the post had gone to someone else by now.

The difference between herself and Dennis, Christine explained, was that she worked on my fine motor skills. So, whereas Dennis might coach me to swing a tennis racquet, Christine might get me to roll a tennis ball along my fingers. I could see the difference, but once again I couldn't see the point. Unless she wanted me to learn how to write with my one functioning big toe.

My scepticism was rising by the minute. Then Dennis returned for my next session and sent it into the stratosphere.

The hour-long course of bending and lifting itself wasn't remarkably different from the previous day's. But what happened afterwards left me stunned. One of the doctors came in near the end to check up on what was happening, watched for five minutes, then announced, 'I'll get an electric wheelchair ordered as soon as possible.'

Dennis nearly dropped my leg. 'Woah,' he said, 'let's not be too hasty.'

The doctor raised an eyebrow. 'Too hasty? What are you saying, Dennis?'

'I'm saying that this guy is going to walk out of here on his own two feet. We're not going to waste a dime on something he'll never need.'

The doctor looked pretty blown away by Dennis's confidence. Melanie nearly fell off her chair.

As for me, I thought this was just Dennis's unsubtle way of trying to get me to push myself harder.

He probably uses the same line with all his patients. But there's no way I'm walking out of here. I'm never walking anywhere again.

These people have never seen a locked-in patient before. I'm pretty sure of that. The doctors can't believe I'm even alive. I can see it in their eyes sometimes. It's like every decision they make is a stab in the dark. I can picture them rushing out to look up everything I say and do to check what might happen next. I'm probably only alive today because of what they've discovered on the internet. They're doing their absolute best, I know that, but I'm just an experiment for them, a research subject they'll discuss one day at a conference.

At least they're realistic, though. My therapists are behaving like I've sprained an ankle. Haven't they read the Wikipedia *page on locked-in syndrome? I won't be walking out of here. I can't even sit upright!*

With the doctors following their own cautious medical path and the various therapists pursuing their much more ambitious goals, I was already facing a two-pronged healthcare attack. Soon, however, a third party joined in.

It was during one of my sister's visits that the idea of alternative medicine first cropped up. Carol believed in it and, in particular, she thought I would benefit from acupuncture. Melanie's ears pricked up at the mention of it and she agreed I should give it a try.

'What have you got to lose?' she said.

She had a point. While I was no devotee of herbal medicines – despite my green fingers – or New Age thinking, I like to think I'm open-minded, so I gave the go-ahead.

Melanie got in touch with Lili immediately, and she plotted a path through the various administrative hoops that needed to be negotiated before a private practitioner could be allowed into Care Meridian. Meanwhile, Carol set about finding the acupuncturist.

She came up with a remarkable young woman called Sarah whose reputation within the Marin County alternative therapy community couldn't have been higher.

It was all going smoothly, and I was even quite looking forward to my first session with Sarah. Until I saw the size of the needles. Bearing in mind that my body – bar one toe and the limited movement I had in my neck – was utterly inert, and I couldn't yell if I was in pain, I started to have serious second thoughts. Sarah, however, soon charmed and calmed me. She promised I would not feel any pain and insisted that I would feel the benefits instantly. I doubted her on both counts. But then she pointed out that she'd already placed one needle into my toe. I hadn't felt a thing.

Sarah explained the theory behind acupuncture as she worked and it all made perfect sense to me. The needles were designed to enter the body at various energy points, and as all of my nerve endings and muscles had stopped talking to each other, I could see the potential rewards from stimulating them. But was I just being swayed by Sarah's bedside manner? I guessed only time would tell.

We all agreed that I should start to see some results after about twelve visits, so two sessions a week were scheduled for the next six weeks.

One of the other routines I got into at Fairfax was watching TV. It had often been a distraction in the ICU, but now I actively welcomed the chance to lose myself in a programme rather than dwell on what was happening to me – or, rather, not happening. I opted to keep it on twenty-four/seven because waking up alone in the middle of the night could still be terrifying, however comfortable my surroundings were. (John, my roommate, had been moved to his own room about a week after I'd arrived.) The only

problem was that I needed a nurse to change the channels. But with my call button within easy reach of my head, which I could now move to the side with a bit of concentration, even that didn't pose a problem.

Watching TV provided a good opportunity to work on the various exercises Dennis and the other therapists had prescribed for me over the past couple of weeks. It was easier to relax without the pressure of my 'teachers' watching over me, and I certainly had plenty of time on my hands. But day after day, night after night, nothing happened.

Then, late one night while I was propped up on my pillow, staring at the TV, I managed to move my left leg. I'd been trying to do it for so long that when it finally happened it came as a massive shock. But I wasn't imagining it. It definitely rotated sideways on my command.

I couldn't believe it, especially as this was my bad leg, the one with the clot, the one that had received far less attention than the other. But here it was, lolling left, then lolling right, precisely when I told it to.

Was it thanks to the needles? Was it going to happen after the toe? All I knew for sure is that I wanted to shout the house down. In fact, I started to move my head towards the call button. But then I stopped myself. This news could wait until I saw the person I wanted to share it with most. And, for once, that wasn't Lili.

It was Dennis.

To his credit, he'd never once been anything but positive in front of me. And he'd needed to be. After nearly three weeks with no results, as far as I could tell, the doctors were starting to lose hope. But Dennis had just kept trying, had kept insisting that something would happen eventually.

And now it had.

He was predictably over the moon when he learned what I'd achieved. His response was equally predictable, too. This was just the starting point of my rehab, not the end. In fact, rather than let me bask in my success, he intensified my programme.

While I would remain in bed during the sessions with Kahlin and Christine, Dennis's were now to take place in a recuperation room. What happened there was going to be arduous, I knew that. In fact, just getting there was hell.

I watched as a tall, crane-like structure on wheels was pushed into the room. Long feet at the bottom stuck out like the tines of a forklift truck. Dangling from the arm at the top was a rubber harness. The whole contraption looked like the kind of machine a mechanic would employ to lift out a car's engine.

What it didn't look like was something that could lift me. At least not comfortably.

'Say hello to the hoyer lift,' Dennis said proudly. Then, talking me through the process as effervescently as ever, he rolled me onto one side and slipped half the harness underneath my butt. Then he rolled me the other way to finish the job. Next he attached the cables from crane to the harness and, after a brief warning, pressed a button.

It was a slow process but none the better for that. One minute I was lying almost flat in my bed; the next I was suspended above it, like a piñata dangling from a tree and just as vulnerable.

I could deal with the discomfort. It was the humiliation that was making me burn with rage. I wasn't being winched to safety by a helicopter. I was being lifted out of bed. What's more, Dennis wasn't just transferring me to a gurney. He planned to take me all the way to the rehab suite on the other side of the building like this. I don't know how long it took, but every second of being wheeled down those hallways, trussed up like a bad guy in Spider-Man's net, I just wanted to cry. The ignominy of having Arthur wipe my ass every day was nothing compared with this in terms of sheer debasement. For all the good work he'd already done and promised to do in the future, I hated Dennis that day.

By the time we reached the therapy room I wasn't in the mood to do anything. Dennis, of course, had other ideas.

I was met with the sight of a padded platform, about two feet off the ground. It could be used as a bed or tilted up as a chair. After manoeuvring the hoyer lift next to it, Dennis lowered me down. The crane still held my weight, and by manipulating my legs he managed to get me into a sitting position.

After more than a month on my back, it felt good to be upright. But only for a few minutes. At first I thought my feeding tube must be digging into me, but then I realised my stomach muscles were screaming. They hadn't been used for so long that they'd forgotten what to do. The longer I sat there, the more wobbly I felt. Gradually, though, Dennis loosened the grip of the harness and before I knew it I was sitting up on my own. Yes, my spine was against a padded backrest, but I wasn't tipping over.

That almost made the shame of the hoyer chair worthwhile.

Almost . . .

We did exactly the same thing over the next few days until one afternoon Dennis scooped me out of bed as usual but didn't take me to the therapy room. Instead, he lowered me into a wheelchair, confident that I wouldn't double over. That might seem like a small step, but it opened up a whole new world for me. The world outside my room.

'Okay, Rich, where would you like to go?'

I wished I had some control of my mouth. Not just to say 'thank you' to my marvellously persistent and patient therapist, but to smile. My expression hadn't changed in so long that I'd forgotten what it felt like. I still couldn't manage that, but as I took in the sights of the Care Meridian hallways, I did something else I hadn't experienced for a very long time.

I cried.

Just feeling a warm tear on my cheek was another reason to smile. After the beating my masculinity had taken recently, I wasn't afraid of this little show of emotion. I was simply overjoyed by what it signified. Something else was working!

The wheelchair felt like a stretch limo to me, I was so happy to be sitting upright rather than lying on my back. Everyone we passed told me they were pleased to see me looking so well. I still had tubes coming out of every orifice, but I knew what they meant.

We finally reached a set of glass double doors at the back of the building. Through them I could see grass and flowers and trees. It had been so long. By the time Dennis had opened the doors and I was actually out there, with the aromas of the plants and freshly mown lawn filtering through to my nostrils, I was in heaven. And that was even before I registered the sun's rays caressing my face and arms. I will remember that moment for ever. I felt like I was experiencing the sounds, the sensations and the colours for the first time.

It could have been raining, the lawn could have been covered in mud, the flower beds could have been full of weeds. I wouldn't even have minded if the grounds were being used as a garbage tip by the neighbourhood. After thinking for so long that I would never see anything other than a TV screen again, I was just so grateful to be outside. More than inhaling the sweet aromas of the flowers and gazing at the expansive blueness of the sky, being in the garden gave me something else. It gave me the courage to dream, the strength to imagine that I could – *would* – have a life outside of Care Meridian's walls. I just had to want it enough.

And I really did want it now.

But then something started to go wrong. The sky started to darken. The green of the grass turned to grey. The red, yellow and mauve of the flowers disappeared. I heard my name being called over and over again from someone a long, long way away.

Then everything turned to black.

CHAPTER EIGHTEEN

Hi, Babe

So, I guess I've died.

Why have I been fighting against this for so long? It's not so bad. It's peaceful, actually. No bright lights, no noises, no torture machines. I like it. It's just a shame I didn't have a chance to say goodbye. I wish I could have …

Wait a minute, is that someone calling me?

Who even knows I'm here?

I woke up back in bed. After so long on my back the rush of blood from my head being upright in the wheelchair had been too much for me. I had only fainted, but Dennis didn't know that. It must have been scary for him. Scarier than it was for me, anyway.

After that incident, for obvious reasons, Dennis decided to scale back his programme. For the next week I remained in bed and we resumed our old set of motion exercises. I also continued to work with Christine and Kahlin. Compared with my progress with Dennis, they appeared to be banging their heads against a brick wall, but they both assured me it was only a matter of time.

I just wished I shared their confidence.

I was bedridden again, aside from when Margarita took me for my whirlpool baths, but at least that meant I avoided the horrors of the hoyer lift. I know that vanity should have been the last thing on my mind, but my ego had taken a kicking every time Dennis had hoisted me up there. Whatever was left of my manhood had virtually disappeared the first time he scooped me up. If I ever got the chance to assert some semblance of authority, I swore I would take it.

I didn't have to wait long for the opportunity. It wasn't the way I would have chosen to make a stand, but at that moment it was all I had.

It began when I noticed the familiar rumbling in my belly as my bowels prepared for an evacuation. (I apologise, but there's no nice way to describe this!)

Oh, great. Just what I need. More humiliation.

But this time there was another sensation, too. Something I distantly remembered. If I really concentrated, I could make the rumbling stop.

I think I've got control of my bowels again.

It must have been related to all the core muscle work I'd been doing with Dennis before I'd passed out. Perhaps I'd ask someone later. Right then, all that mattered was flexing this newly awoken muscle in the only way I knew how. An hour later, I still hadn't had a movement. Another hour passed and still nothing. I was holding it in for as long as I could. Like my life depended on it.

It's no criticism of the medical staff that they didn't pick up on what I was doing at first. I suppose each nurse and carer assumed one of the others had changed my diaper. Or perhaps they didn't keep track of my intestinal activity at all – just routinely checked and changed me if necessary. To be honest, I didn't care.

I had no idea where I intended to go with this 'clean protest'. I just thought that after all the humiliations of the previous few weeks, a bit of pain and discomfort would be a price worth paying for a day or two without a young man or woman cleaning my ass.

I could not have been more wrong.

Eventually, Arthur realised I hadn't had a movement for some time. He asked me whether I was holding it in and, knowing the game was up, I blinked once. While he was happy that I had regained some control, he was cross that I'd been so stupid. Indeed, by then, so was I. I'd held it in for so long I'd made myself constipated. Even when I tried to go nothing happened.

What followed was far worse than being cleaned or carried through the corridors in the hoyer lift. In fact, being cleaned *while* being transported in the hoyer could not have been any more degrading – for either of us.

To try to break the impasse, Arthur rolled me on my side and inserted a suppository. I knew it hadn't worked when I heard him sigh. Where did that leave us? Unfortunately, it left me on my side and Arthur with his fingers inside my butt as he performed a digital disimpaction. It wasn't particularly painful, but I'd never felt shame like it. That poor man was scraping the crap out of my backside and all because of my petty pride. I was just relieved I couldn't see his face while he did it.

I'm sure Arthur took it all in his stride, but it left me emotionally scarred.

'Don't be so silly next time,' he warned me as he cleaned up.

I didn't need to be told twice.

I've never been the sort of guy who needs to remind everyone how much of a man he is. I work out because I like it, not because I think it makes me look 'masculine'. I ride motorcycles for the same reason. And I joined the Police Department because I wanted to help my community, not to throw my weight around. I don't have an ego where being 'a man' is concerned.

Or so I used to think. If that were true, then I wouldn't mind being swung around in the hoyer lift like a goldfish in a bag, would I? And I wouldn't play such stupid games with my bowel movements, either. Why did I try to hold it in, if not to show I'm still a man in control of his body?

I'm not proud of what I did. But it's not the whole story. There was another reason for pulling that stunt: I don't like imposing on people. If I could have made Arthur's day easier by not soiling my diaper, then that would have been a good thing. My mistake was failing to consider that what I was doing might make his day much harder. And that upsets me, so much so that I feel a tear running down my cheek. I weep whenever Lili or Melanie or Shannon leaves at the end of the evening, too.

I don't care who sees me. I know it doesn't make me any less of a man.

Things were happening. My right leg was starting to twitch into life just as my left had done a week or so earlier. Even my speech therapist, Kahlin, was beginning to get somewhere. After weeks of no progress we'd reduced my sessions from an hour a day to one every other day. Rather than being fazed by the failure to achieve any of her goals, I think Kahlin was more concerned about me losing hope. And she was right to be worried. Day after day, week after week, speaking again seemed like a futile dream. But then everything changed one afternoon when she arrived and asked me how I was.

I looked across to my spell board, which was her cue to pick it up, and a few minutes later she was staring at what she'd written in the blank space in the middle:

M. Y. T. O. N. G. U. E. M. O. V. E. D.

A smile spread across her face. 'Did it now?' she asked. 'Okay, let's take a look.'

With expert gentleness she pulled my jaw open and peered inside.

'Care to try again, Rich?'

I focused everything I had on the muscles at the root of my mouth. Being so much closer to my brain, it felt like I should be able to control my tongue more easily than my leg. In fact, it was like lifting weights. While I felt I could do it, the energy it demanded was shattering.

Then, suddenly, I felt a twitch. There was definite movement and, from the even wider beam on Kahlin's lips, I could tell she'd spotted it too.

We both hoped that this signalled the start of a fairly rapid improvement. The major problem was the trach pipe. It was impossible to speak without air. And while the little balloon blocked my windpipe, that was not going to change. On top of that, the balloon stopped me eating normally, of course. Still, Kahlin said, the trach pipe wouldn't be there for ever. In the mean-time I needed to start exercising my tongue. Like every other part of my body, it was a muscle sorely in need of development.

So far, so good. But then I panicked as Kahlin reached over to my cabinet and returned with a small handheld mirror.

'I think if you can see your tongue you'll be able to control it more easily.'

No!

Plenty of time had passed by now, but I still felt exactly the same as I had at The Queen. I didn't want any mirrors pointing in my direction. However good my progress had been, I did not want to see myself in that state. But how could I tell Kahlin that?

I tried looking over at the spell board as urgently as possible. Unfortunately, Kahlin only had eyes for the mirror. That left me no choice. As soon as she got the small silver circle lined up in front my face, I closed my eyes. It was all I could do. My only weapon.

'Rich?' Kahlin asked after a few seconds. 'Are you okay?'

I opened my eyes, blinked twice, then fixed them firmly shut again. I was prepared to stay like that permanently, if necessary.

Luckily, Kahlin got the message.

'Do you have a problem with using a mirror?'

Another rapid blink, then back to closed.

'If you don't want to see yourself, I understand that. We can find other ways to work.'

I felt her place the mirror calmly on the bed, like a cop giving up his weapon at gunpoint. Only then did I open my eyes again.

'It was a silly idea, anyway,' Kahlin said. 'Let's see what else we can do.'

It turned out that, over time, there was a whole lot more that Kahlin could do. From being the therapist with the least to play with, she now introduced new *daily* exercises that were designed to prepare me to speak and swallow. Each tiny exercise was as gruelling as anything Dennis could come up with, and I was just as exhausted when they ended. It didn't help that I still couldn't see the point of them.

Yes, I could move my tongue, but my jaw was a locked safe. In fact, I was convinced it had been permanently damaged by the rubber block that had first propped it open, which hardly gave me confidence that it would soon be back under my control.

It doesn't matter what I learn to do with my tongue. Unless I want a new career as a ventriloquist, it won't amount to a hill of beans.

Despite Kahlin's optimism, another bleak night alone with my darkest thoughts lay ahead of me. I spent the small hours mulling over my inevitably silent life. My silent, sedentary, weak life.

As depressing as such thoughts sometimes were, I never lost faith that I would leave Care Meridian. My only doubts were to do with my quality of life once I had left. Come each morning and each new therapy session, however, I was never anything but committed. Perhaps that was the reason why during one speech session I suddenly realised my chin was moving away from my nose. I was moving my mouth. My jaw was working after all.

Naturally, Kahlin had exercises to exploit this latest development. Then she took it a stage further by presenting me with something called a Passy-Muir valve. With the balloon still blocking my windpipe, I was unable to pass air over my vocal cords, which made making sounds virtually impossible. But the Passy-Muir was designed to work with the trach pipe to allow the user to draw air into his mouth and, ultimately, speak.

I couldn't wait to give it a try, but, boy, was it hard work. Breathing through a trach pipe was not something I would ever wish on anyone, but trying to get a tune out of this new valve seemed almost impossible. Drawing a single breath took so much effort I questioned whether the valve was even open.

'The point of this is to get your diaphragm working strongly enough that we'll be able to remove the trach pipe,' Kahlin explained. 'We'll build up to it, but the target is seventy-two hours. When you can use it for that long, that's the cue for the trach pipe to come out.'

Even as I listened to her explaining it to me, my eyes were almost popping out of my skull with the effort of trying.

I'll be lucky to get up to seventy-two seconds . . .

Every step forward seemed to be accompanied by a step back, and not only with Kahlin. When Dennis decided it was time for me to try the wheelchair again, we discovered a new problem. I was in it for only five, ten and then fifteen minutes at a time, but because I'd lost so much weight and had virtually no meat on my butt, I found it really uncomfortable to sit down. Even with a cushion on the leather seat I still wanted to keep adjusting my weight, which, of course, was something I couldn't do.

With my rear end unable to take the pressure, Dennis stepped up his work on my legs, which involved my introduction to another device in the therapy room. This was far more intimidating than the sitting table and, once again, a trip in the hoyer was required for me even to reach it.

The 'standing board' was a piece of kit that looked and felt like a funfair attraction. I'd seen circus acts where a woman is strapped to a vertical board and spun around while knives are thrown all around her. This felt just like that. I was lowered down until I was flat on my back and strapped to the board with my feet aligned to some small plastic ledges. There were also sidebars, which my arms were hooked over. The whole contraption looked like a giant walker on its side. When Dennis was confident everything was in place, he threw a switch and I found myself starting to tilt up, and up, and up. The walker was going vertical.

I was fastened to the board so I couldn't fall forwards, but feeling my body weight bearing down on my legs was the most painful thing I'd experienced for ages, even though I was fifty pounds lighter than I used to be. It was as though my leg muscles had dissolved. Even my bones were struggling to keep me pointing in the right direction. I think I lasted five minutes, if that. When the board started to tilt back, I thought I would cry with relief.

But Dennis was in no mood to let the momentum drop. Five minutes was still five minutes. A month – even a week – earlier and I would have been jelly. As it was, I was just extremely weak. Every day we went back to the same machine to build up my strength.

He devised another exercise for me, too. On paper, this one sounded easier. It didn't take long for me to learn that it was anything but.

Sadly for my skinny butt, Dennis saw the wheelchair as a valuable tool not only to get me sitting, but to get me walking. Now that I had some control over both legs, Dennis brought in an exercise device that was basically just the pedals and sprockets from a bicycle mounted on a box. With the wheelchair brake applied, I could sit and put my legs on the pedals. At first, with Dennis's help, I could manage no more than a couple of limp rotations. By the end of the week, I could do five minutes on my own. Dennis's goal was two hours every day in the wheelchair combined with as much pedalling as possible. I think the most I ever managed was forty-five minutes. But a few months earlier, even that, like standing up, would have been out of the question. I was undoubtedly making significant progress with my legs.

If only my arms would respond in the same way.

I was starting to give up hope, so it was a considerable shock when I finally felt a twitch in my fingers. It was less of a surprise that this happened in my left hand, rather than my right. The same pattern I'd experienced with my legs was repeating itself. When I'd first started to regain movement in my left leg the doctors had told me that the right side of the brain controls the left side of the body, and vice versa, so clearly the clot in my brain stem had impaired my left hemisphere more than my right.

Even so, I didn't expect it to take so long for my right hand to come back on line – or for it to look so damned weird. Despite its elevation, there seemed to be some kind of build-up in it. To me, it looked like an inflated Marigold washing-up glove – five weak and puffy finger shapes swollen up like unpricked sausages. The doctors just said it was normal and promised they'd monitor it.

Secretly, though, I don't think they could believe what they were seeing, and not just with respect to my hand. Although my progress might have seemed fairly slow, given the condition in which I'd arrived, it was sensational. The notes attached to my case when I'd entered Care Meridian predicted such a low chance of recovery that they'd just been intent on keeping me alive. Yet now I was recovering – and in ways they hadn't budgeted for. Not only was I the first locked-in patient they'd treated, but according to all the case studies they'd read over the past few weeks, I was mending at a faster rate than any sufferer in history.

Almost every day they had some new and unexpected development to assess and try to explain.

They continued to monitor my right hand for another two weeks before finally there was some movement. It wasn't much, but I was definitely able to twitch my fingers. By contrast, I could already form an 'okay' sign with the forefinger and thumb of my left hand. Christine, my occupational therapist, couldn't have been prouder. I couldn't wait for a chance to surprise my loved ones with it.

Even though Lili wasn't present every day now, she joined me in celebrating each new physical advance. She was also busy plotting my future and making provisions for every eventuality. As usual, she did that with all the efficiency and professionalism she'd displayed ever since I'd been admitted to The Queen. I'd needed her to remain strong, and to some extent that meant she had to be detached and clinical. But the next time I saw her she brought up a topic I really didn't want to face.

'Right, you know I have power of attorney,' she said.

I blinked once, but wondered where she was going with this.

'But what if something happens to me?'

What do you mean? You're eight years younger than me and, if anything, even fitter than I've ever been.

As I said, every time I took a step forwards, something seemed to drag me back. I was stupefied that she'd even mentioned it. The idea of a life without Lili just didn't bear thinking about. Without her, I was certain I wouldn't have made it as far as I had.

'We need to be sensible about this, Rich. I have to drive a lot of miles to get here . . .'

Tell me about it!

' . . . and anything could happen to me on that road. So I think we should nominate one of your daughters to assume power of attorney should anything happen to me.'

She was determined to resolve the matter immediately, so, using the spell board, we agreed on Shannon. Later that afternoon, Lili asked her and a few days later she came in with a notary public – a lawyer who deals with non-contentious civil issues – and a stack of papers. Most of them were for Shannon and Lili to sign. But obviously we hit a stumbling block when it came to me adding my signature.

'You'll have to make do with an "X",' Lili told the lawyer.

'Is that really the best you can do?' he asked.

Lili pointed to my still swollen hand. 'I think it's a miracle we can even get that.'

Somehow they managed to insert a pen between my inflated claws. Gingerly, and with all my concentration focused on my hand, I dragged the ballpoint across the page. One line down. Lift and move across. Then one line up. Not perfect, but undoubtedly an 'X'. Fortunately, the lawyer was happy, especially as he'd witnessed it himself.

'Congratulations, Mr Marsh. That's all in order.'

It had all gone smoothly, but I could barely look at Lili after our legal visitor had left. How could she even suggest that she might die? I was the one on Death Row. Or, rather, I had been. I was finally starting to accept that things were going my way. Even so, I decided that if the possibility of a future apart was playing on

her mind, then I had to do something about it. And the best thing
I could do was get better, or at least as well as my body allowed me
to be. If Dennis thought I would one day be able to shuffle around
with a walker, then I had to believe it, too.

Because it wasn't just my future riding on it.

*I really enjoy the weekends here, because I know I'll get to see Lili. If she
arrives early enough, the nurse lets her shave me. It's a nice little intimacy
we get to share. It lets me know I'm still half of a couple. Not a freak show
to be pitied.*

Unfortunately, there was a downside to weekends, too. Dennis
worked Monday to Friday, so I was pretty much confined to my
room for forty-eight hours, and I missed our trips around the corridors.

But then, one Saturday, Arthur asked Lili if she would like to
take me out for a while. In the wheelchair.

Lili could scarcely control her excitement and started asking
what she needed to do. Arthur said he'd take care of getting me
into the chair, but then Lili would have to do the pushing. She
looked like she couldn't wait.

Although I relished the prospect of some alone time outside
the room with Lili, part of me thought she shouldn't have to lug
me around. Even on wheels and fifty pounds lighter than I'd been
at my peak, I was still heavy. Dennis was a fit man but even he had
to put his back into shifting me on anything other than a gurney.
It wasn't right that my wife had to do this.

And yet, once I'd got over the embarrassment of being
winched out of bed and into the chair, I had to admit the change
of scenery was refreshing. By the time we reached the outside
patio, I was close to being positively happy. The fresh air and

September sunshine on my face were so welcome. The only draw-back was that Lili was standing behind me, so I had no means of communicating with her. Only once we'd stopped did she come and sit on a chair next to me. I forgot where I was, and why I was there, for a second. Me and Lili, my wife and I, were together alone in the great outdoors. It was almost romantic.

Those brief couple of hours gave me fresh impetus to work on my recovery as hard as I could.

Once Lili had left and I was back on my own in the room I began to question my need for the trach pipe. With my tongue moving and my diaphragm working, it just seemed to be holding me back. Even though the longest I'd managed to work with the Passy-Muir valve had been only thirty-six hours – about half the target – I was confident that breathing for real was well within my grasp.

As I told Melanie via the spell board, if the doctors allowed me to breathe through my mouth again, I would be able to push my body harder in the physical therapy sessions and we would see faster, greater improvements everywhere. She agreed and went off to find a doctor and put my idea to him. When she returned she said they were considering it.

It was the next morning before I heard what they really thought. One of the doctors came up to my bedside and said, 'I think I know a bit more about these things than you do.' He was completely unimpressed by my logic and indeed by my progress with the valve. 'The trach pipe stays in.'

It was his tone that annoyed me more than his decision. Obviously, as a result, I couldn't wait to prove him wrong. But how was I going to do that?

A few days later I thought I'd managed it when Arthur came in and said, 'It's your lucky day. I've been told to unplug you.'

Wow! The doc has changed his mind. I knew I didn't need the trach pipe.

But Arthur wasn't reaching for the tube in my throat.

I was no stranger to having my catheter removed. I was on my third in six weeks. The previous two had got infected and had begun to hurt. But no bug was as painful as having the plastic fan shape yanked through your penis. I knew what to expect and braced myself, but it was still agony. The only difference was that I wasn't getting a replacement this time.

So what was I meant to do now?

Like everything else, I was told the longer you use something as a crutch, the harder it is to give it up. There was only one way to get my urinary muscles functioning properly again, and that was to use them. Or *try* to use them. Just as a twitch in my leg hadn't meant I could suddenly walk again, the fact that I could feel my urine stream didn't mean I could control it.

So it came as no surprise to anyone when I soiled my pants later that day. By then, Care Meridian had been allowing me to dress in shorts and a T-shirt for some time. Even with a diaper underneath, I was much more comfortable in my own clothes rather than a medical gown, especially once Dennis started wheeling me around the facility. Whatever you're wearing is of little consequence, however, if you don't have control of your bladder – and your diaper has been left unpinned.

At first I just had to let nature take its course and go in the diaper. But after a few days a little more feeling returned and I started to realise in advance when I needed to empty my bladder. If I was lucky, I could hit the call button and someone would appear. Sadly, though, by the time they'd run through the list of questions and had worked out why I was calling it was usually too late.

It was about a week before we started to make some real

progress. I was rolled on my side and given a little hand-held urinal. When I felt the urge, I could move my left hand just enough to get the little bottle to my penis. There were still more misses than hits at first, but it was certainly worth persevering. If I hit the call button before I started, Arthur, Brenda or Margarita would appear, see what I was trying to do, and help out.

My right hand was still little more than a puffy paperweight at this stage, but my left was improving every day. As well as the numerous fine motor skills that are required to do something as simple as move a bottle a couple of inches, I was developing some arm strength. Again, my biggest breakthrough came when I was on my own, but when my family arrived the next day I was quick to show them that I could now touch my nose. I couldn't pinch it, or even pick it, but I could reach it for the first time in months.

I felt like I'd won an Olympic medal.

Because of her work commitments, Lili didn't get to see many of my achievements the moment they happened. In a way, it was nice to work at them and then surprise her by casually signalling 'okay' or touching my nose, but I think she would have preferred to share some of my joy when I struggled to do something for the first time. She missed my next major breakthrough, too, although Melanie was there to witness it. This time, however, it didn't feel much like a breakthrough. In fact, at first I thought it was going to kill me.

I was sitting up in bed, as usual at the standard thirty-five degrees. I don't know what started it, but all of a sudden I was coughing. And coughing. And really, really coughing. Melanie leapt out of her seat to try to calm me down but there was a tickle in my throat that just would not clear, and drinking a glass of water, of course, was out of the question. The harder I coughed, the more my whole body convulsed with the effort.

At that point I felt my trach pipe ping halfway out of my throat.

As soon as she saw it, Melanie dived for the call button. The doctor arrived within minutes, but rather than jump to my bedside and push the tube back in, he stood back and assessed the situation. Meanwhile, I was still coughing.

'Did you pull this out on purpose?' he asked me, clearly unimpressed.

I shook my head. And blinked twice just to emphasise the point.

'Well,' he said, leaning in to listen to my chest, 'you seem to be breathing okay without it.' Finally he reached for the tube, but he still didn't push it back in. Instead, he pulled it out completely.

'Thanks,' I said.

The voice was scarcely identifiable as mine. It sounded more like it belonged to a small, frail child. And it had taken all my energy to say that single word. But the astonished expression it generated on the doctor's face and, more than that, the way Melanie's eyes filled with tears will stay with me for ever.

I'm speaking!

However, I knew their reactions would be nothing compared with that of the person who mattered to me most. It would be a long night before I could share the good news with her, but I hoped it would be worth the wait.

I swore Melanie to secrecy and practised my sounds all night. I planned to play it cool in the morning but when the time came I couldn't hold back. The second Lili walked through the door I didn't even wait for her to look at me. I didn't need to any more.

'Hi, babe,' I said.

The rest is a tearful blur.

CHAPTER NINETEEN

Let's Walk

I. Can. Speak.

Learning to speak again was one of the most fulfilling journeys of my life. Communicating for three and a half months with only my eyelids and a spell board had taken its toll. Would I have traded the ability to speak for mobility? At one time I would have answered a resolute 'yes'. I was a loner. I didn't use many words at the best of times. But almost a third of a year without being able to tell my loved ones how I felt about them had been torture.

I threw myself into Kahlin's new exercises but there was a downside to having the trach pipe removed. With the hole in my windpipe stitched up, I could no longer be suctioned, which meant I needed to learn how to swallow. And that wasn't as straightforward as it might sound. As my body struggled to find its natural balance, my saliva glands seemed to be producing liquid by the mugful – apparently a common side-effect among post-trach patients – and, with my throat so out of practice, I really struggled to cope.

I was warned that failure to clear my throat could lead to

phlegm in my lungs and possibly pneumonia. And that, for a man in my frail condition, could prove fatal.

The only problem was, I just could not keep up. Kahlin gave me a box of tissues so I could wipe up the overflow, but the secretions showed no sign of slowing. By the second day I had half filled the litter sack tied to my bed rail, and within a week I'd got through three boxes of tissues. At nighttime the torrent subsided a little, so I was in less danger. During the day, however, the floodgates opened so wide that I questioned whether they would ever close again.

It doesn't matter how good my swallowing becomes, no one could drink this amount.

On the plus side, at least I could now reach my mouth quite easily and swab its wet walls. I was still using my left hand, and my close control wasn't great, but I could do enough to dab, fold and discard a soggy tissue. Anything that required more dexterity was still beyond me, and that included using the television remote. When Arthur first placed the little device next to my left hand, I was able to rest a finger on the channel- or volume-change button, but pressing them was trickier. Unable to grasp the remote, I just stabbed my fingers down on the tiny buttons – and then watched the whole unit spring into the air and flip over. Turning the remote the right way up was straightforward enough, but then I faced the same problem. I didn't have the strength to hold the rectangular box and press down any of the buttons at the same time as that involved applying pressure in two directions at once. As with so much else, the TV still seemed to be out of my control.

Overnight I dwelt on the problem. By morning I thought I had a solution, but I would need a little help.

When Arthur came in that morning I managed to convey to

him, feebly, that I would like to see the facility's handyman, if he wasn't too busy.

'That's a strange request, but I'll see what I can do.'

With a curious Arthur watching, I asked the handyman – through a mixture of words, sounds, hand gestures and the spell board – if he could cut a piece of wood about a foot long, three inches wide and an inch thick, then attach the remote control to it with Velcro.

'That shouldn't be a problem,' he said.

It was another tick in the customer-care column for Care Meridian when the handyman returned within half an hour. He placed the whole package on the bed next to me, then joined Melanie and Arthur to see what I planned to do with it. The board acted as ballast, so no matter how ham-fisted and off target my pressure, the remote would not flip and I was able to change channels.

It was a minor success but it meant a lot to me because I now had full control over the TV. It was the first time in three and a half months that I could say that about anything. I didn't need to ring any bells in the middle of the night or have to endure programmes I couldn't stand. I could just prod a button and change everything. It was my first little glimpse of a future in which I wouldn't be reliant on others for everything. I was reasserting my independence.

In addition to the thrill of being able to channel hop, the very act of solving my own problem was immensely satisfying. In fact, it made me feel alive again. Not just living but, for the first time since I'd arrived at Care Meridian, *thriving*. Now I needed to capitalise on that spirit. Whatever it took to reach the next level, I had to do it. After all, I'd wanted the trach pipe removed because that would allow me to work harder.

Fortunately, with Dennis's next session never more than a few hours away, I soon had the opportunity to put my newfound resolve to the test. For the first time, I didn't moan when he gave me the bike pedals to push. I just got down to it and did forty-five minutes straight off. Dennis smiled.

From then on I pedalled day after day, and I spent ever more time strapped to the standing board. Dennis also gave me arm exercises to do while I was upright to increase my upper-body muscle. Each time, I pushed myself to achieve greater endurance. The incentive of getting home and maybe having control of *my own* TV was a carrot that was proving increasingly irresistible. Work, work, work, work. I had virtually lived in the gym in my former life. I just needed to treat this like another exercise programme.

I could see the pride in Dennis's face the day I managed forty minutes on the standing board. The following day I achieved the same again, but that left me disappointed. I wanted more.

'Let's go for forty-five minutes this time, Dennis,' I said, my voice straining to be heard over the aircon unit.

Dennis started to answer but stopped himself. I swear I saw a plan beginning to form in his mind.

'I've got a better idea,' he said as his smile broadened. 'Give me a minute.'

I watched, intrigued, as he walked to the back of the room and returned with a tall, white, cage-like structure. Of its four legs, the two at the front were on wheels while the two at the back had thick rubber stoppers. I recognised it as a walker, a device used by the frail and infirm to support their weight while taking steps.

But what use is that for me?

I guess it's a type of denial. When you think you're at one place on a chart and your teacher thinks you're somewhere else, you don't see what's in front of your face. Clearly, Dennis felt I'd built up sufficient strength on the pedal machine and the standing board for us take the next step. Or, rather, for me to take it. However small, however slow, that was what he wanted from me now. The promise he'd made all those weeks ago when he'd refused the offer of an electric wheelchair was about to be tested for the first time.

Unlike those of conventional walkers, the frame of this one came all the way up to my elbows to offer full support. I could never see myself being able to use the lower device, with the grips around waist height, but even the one Dennis was carrying seemed a wildly optimistic idea.

Dennis disagreed. 'Today, Rich, you are going to walk.'

'Oh, man,' I wheezed. 'I don't know if I'm ready for this.'

He looked me directly in the eyes. 'You are ready, Rich. You just have to believe it.'

I don't know the statistics about the power of positive thinking, but I do know that Dennis and his colleagues' enthusiasm was contagious. Without their unflinching support I would still be in Care Meridian to this day.

He brought the walker as close to the standing board as possible, then, taking my full weight in his arms, eased me across to it. The high metal frame meant I could rest my arms without having to grip too hard. The majority of my weight, however, was still going to be supported by my legs. It was just like the standing board except there were no straps to hold me in place. If I buckled now, it would be up to my arms to catch me.

'I'm here,' Dennis said, reading my mind as usual. 'You're not gonna need me, but I'm right here if you do.'

The walker was pointing towards the door, about ten feet away. Four months earlier, I could have reached it in two or three strides. As it was, I was looking around for the hoyer lift. Suddenly, it didn't seem such a bad way of getting around after all.

No, I have to do this. At the very least, I have to try …

I'd been standing for a month now. Yes, I'd been strapped to a board. And, yes, some of my weight had been supported by those straps the whole time. And, yes, I'd been perfectly still. But looking down at my feet on the grey, rubber-matted floor, I was confident I could build on what I'd achieved, prop myself up on the walker and stay there for almost an hour.

That wasn't enough for Dennis, though. The plan had changed.

'Come on. It's time for us to go,' he said, more quietly than I'd ever heard him, and more serious. 'Let's walk.'

He's saying 'us' but he means 'you'. I'm the only one who can do this …

I thought about the brain signals I needed to send to my legs to make the muscles down there twitch. Then I imagined doing more than twitching. I pictured my stronger left leg lifting and swinging forwards while I shifted my weight to the right side of my body, to my arms and my other leg. In my mind I saw it make contact with the floor and prepare to take my weight.

Now I just have to do it …

Nothing happened.

'Focus on the foot, Rich,' said Dennis. 'Lift your foot. Just lift it and let it fall forwards.'

The words were still ringing in my ears when I felt my right side getting heavy. That could mean only one thing. My left leg must be off the ground. Half smiling, half grimacing, I was as much a spectator as Dennis was as my left leg swung towards the front of the walker. My body lurched in the same direction and I paused as the metal cage took my weight. But I didn't buckle. It was fine. *I* was fine.

Now for the tricky one.

My right leg had come back on line so much later than my left that I wasn't surprised it hadn't naturally, instinctively, wanted to move first. But it was ready now. With a gargantuan effort I guided it towards its partner.

It landed like a meteor crashing into a desert but I stayed upright. All that was left now was to use my newly strengthened core muscles to ease the walker's wheels forwards. It hurt – every inch from my groin to my chest – but I managed it. The whole cage rolled forwards, maybe only eight inches, but enough to make me smile. To make *us* smile.

The door was just over nine feet away now.

'I'm doing it,' I rasped. 'I'm walking.'

'Yes, Rich,' Dennis said proudly. 'You really are.'

It took time to get used to controlling my own limbs and manoeuvring the frame. But that was all it took. After I'd covered five feet I was shuffling at ten times the speed I'd set off at.

I thought that reaching the door would be the end of my lesson for the day, so it was a surprise when the fanfare didn't arrive. I turned my head to see Dennis still standing by the standing frame.

'What are you doing over there?' he asked casually. 'Therapy's still got another half an hour to go.'

Bastard.

But I liked his style.

In all, I covered twenty feet, minimum, in around fifteen minutes. I wasn't going to win any land-speed records, but I was deliriously happy. Even as Dennis was helping me back into bed I had a stupid wide grin on my face. My future, I realised, wasn't going to be set at a thirty-five-degree angle for the rest of my life. It was going to be upright. It was going to be mobile. It was going to be as independent as I could make it.

Of course, Lili wasn't there for this great landmark in my recovery. And it was a bit of an anticlimax when I told her about it later. The vulnerable lump of flesh she was looking at in the bed certainly didn't tally with a man who claimed to be walking, albeit with a frame. She would have to see it with her own eyes.

By the time Lili did witness me upright I was managing more than a tentative stroll to the door. Within a couple of weeks, Dennis had me pushing my walker along the corridors and into the lounge area, where there were sofas and chairs for visitors and patients. On my first trip there I passed several of the nurses and doctors who had treated me over the past few months. It was such a small community that we all knew each other well. Even so, I was surprised when the first person I met stopped to pat me on the back. The next did the same. When I reached the reception area the two ladies on the desk stood and applauded me. I felt like a hero. Like a quarterback who'd just won the Superbowl. Everywhere I looked there were cheerleaders encouraging me. They were exactly what I needed. There was no way I could stop, not even for a rest. I couldn't let them down.

It was a landmark for me every time I managed to plant one foot in front of the other, but when I first stepped outside the facility and made my way into the grounds it was my personal equivalent of a lunar landing. I leaned on the walker's tall frame and studied the view. I was there on merit. I'd pushed my walker all the way from my bedside with no help from anyone. I'd pushed and I'd leaned and I'd heaved and eventually I'd walked. I'd got outside entirely under my own steam. One small step for mankind, a giant leap for me.

Without question, regaining some level of mobility was my greatest physical achievement. The walker was big and ugly, but it helped me to get from A to B. Even if I had to use it for the rest of my life, I would take that. Anything was better than lying on my back and relying on other people to fetch everything for me.

Of course, there were consequences to being more active. All that walking, in other words, made me hungry. With my swallowing now under some sort of control, Kahlin decided it was time to introduce what she called 'solid food'. In fact, what I got was yoghurt and mashed banana, neither of which was likely to trouble my teeth. I wasn't able to handle anything as small as cutlery myself, so Kahlin brought the spoon to my lips. I couldn't believe how good it tasted. Not only was it the first thing that had passed my lips for nearly four months, it was so moist. I'd had a craving for liquid for as long as I could remember and this really hit the spot. Unfortunately, though, as tiny as the spoonfuls were, I couldn't manage more than about four mouthfuls before I struggled. I was forced to accept that the feeding tube wouldn't be removed from my stomach any time soon.

Kahlin seemed happy, though. 'I'll get you eating properly in no time,' she promised.

She wouldn't get the chance to keep that promise, however, because on 18 September 2009, after more than three months at Care Meridian, I walked – literally – out of the door for the last time.

Napa here I come . . .

CHAPTER TWENTY

I'd Kill for a Cheeseburger

I hated this journey the last time I made it. It's amazing how your perspective changes when you can see where you're going.

I'm sitting in the passenger seat of the Mustang. Lili's driving, with the same nervous care as a new mother taking her baby home for the first time. The only time she takes her eyes off the road or mirrors is to flick a glance over at me. She's checking if I'm okay.

I've never felt better.

Okay, that's not true. But this is certainly the best I've felt since 19 May. This is the best I've felt since my whole world tipped upside down. I'm looking at the countryside and the birds and the houses as they whizz by and I'm so glad I'm sitting upright again and not lying in the back of an ambulance. I barely even notice my diaper any more, or the food tube coiled inside my shirt.

I'm in a car with my wife and I couldn't be happier.

Even though the last time I'd been there I'd arrived on my back, staring at the sky, I recognised the imposing sight of the Queen of the Valley Medical Center immediately. Almost four months to the day since they'd saved my life, I was back for what I hoped would be the final stage of my treatment. This was the end of the line as far as residential therapy was concerned.

The acute rehab unit is designed, as its name suggests, to prepare patients for life outside the walls of a medical facility. Care
Meridian had started me off on this journey, but now it was acute
rehab's job to get me over the line. Fortunately, I was already at a
relatively good point. I was arriving with movement in all of my
limbs and some ability to walk, speak and eat. They were going to
work on all three areas as hard as they could.

Like everything else in the healthcare sector in the US, it all
came down to money. My medical insurance would cover a two-
week stay, but only on condition that I showed a minimum 25 per
cent improvement at the end of the first week. I had no idea how
they intended to measure that, but I figured they'd try to wriggle
out of the deal if I was even close to missing my target.

I would just have to work hard enough not to give them that
option.

Merely getting me back into The Queen had proved another
significant hurdle for Lili. Yet again, a shortage of beds was the
problem, just as it had been when she'd tried to get me transferred
out of the Facility. Fortunately, though, she knew the head of the
acute rehab unit from the days when she'd worked at the hospital.
That enabled her to bypass the usual admin procedures and deal
directly with him, and she managed to find me a place.

Walking unaided to my room was still beyond me, so a porter
pushed me there in a wheelchair. As we emerged from the eleva-
tor onto the rehab floor I froze. There were at least eight armed
officers outside various rooms along the corridor.

They sure take their security seriously.

I soon learned that the guards weren't there to protect the
patients. The Queen of the Valley has the honour of serving two
local maximum-security prisons, so there were inmates from
Vacaville Penitentiary and San Quentin holed up behind those

doors. Given the shortage of beds, I was relieved to see I got a two-person room to myself. Sharing with a murderer wouldn't be fun for anyone, but for an ex-cop, making small talk across the beds would probably get more than a little awkward.

'Hey, don't I know you?'

Guards or no guards, I'd probably learn to sleep with one eye open pretty quick.

As well as enjoying twice as much space as I'd expected, I was lucky enough to have an en suite bathroom. And it wasn't long before I felt the need to use it. At Care Meridian I would never have made it all the way down the corridor in time, but once I'd been helped out of bed I was now able to use the walker to get inside the little anteroom and pee standing up for the first time since 20 May. Just that simple act of urinating unaided felt unimaginably satisfying. But something else gave me even greater pleasure. Being able to close the door behind me and be on my own, in private, without relying on another soul for any of my needs, albeit for a short period of time, was exquisitely liberating.

I could stay here all day . . .

That sensation of freedom gave me real impetus to work as hard as I could while I was at The Queen. Independence in as many areas of my life as possible had to be my goal.

After the Facility and Care Meridian, I knew what to expect by now. And, sure enough, I was soon shown around the facilities and then introduced to the various therapists and other members of staff. If they were half as skilled as the team at Care Meridian, I knew I would be in safe hands. As it was already late afternoon, there was no time to do anything but acclimatise myself to the regime. The following day, however, would be a different story. The plan was for two half-hour sessions of occupational and physical therapy each day. These would be so intense, I was warned, that any longer would almost certainly be too much for me. Only the speech therapy would last for an hour at a time.

Mike got the ball rolling. He was the head physical therapist and clearly cut from the same cloth as Dennis. Along with his colleague, John, he put me through an early test of my abilities. Then, he promised, he would forget what I *could* do and concentrate on what he thought I *should* be doing.

'Are you up for that?'

'I guess.'

'Let's get started, then.'

The first thing Mike did was replace my high walker with a standard-level one. The motion stayed the same but the pressure on my wrists and hands increased tenfold. Naturally, I transferred the weight I could no longer support with my arms onto my legs. So in one fell swoop I was now working all four limbs harder.

Walking was the fulcrum of Mike's programme. First we covered every communal inch of the rehab unit's floor. Then we went outside and got more ambitious. The path from the main entrance was on a sweeping incline, but Mike insisted I was up to it. Going down was exhausting enough. Turning and climbing back up seemed to take for ever.

In addition to improving my walking in general, Mike had several very specific targets he wanted me to meet. I was proud that I could go to the bathroom unaided, but I still needed help to get out of bed. So Mike helped me onto a padded bench and worked me through a series of exercises designed to replicate the movements I'd need to get to my feet on my own. As I said, my stay in acute rehab wasn't designed to mend me completely. It was intended to help me negotiate the hurdles I would face in my day-to-day life back at home. The rest I could work on once I was there.

Back at home! Just the thought of our little house on East Avenue sent a shiver up my spine. Was I being naïvely optimistic? Was there really a chance that I would make it back to Alta Heights?

If I worked hard, I was sure there was. There had to be.

Focusing on that thought, I forced myself to do whatever Mike and John demanded, and more. After they introduced me to the free weights and recumbent bike in the therapy gym, I asked if I could use them outside my scheduled sessions. I was not going to let any insurance company say I did not deserve another week there.

I was just as keen to practise the skills my occupational therapist, Paul, outlined for me. Again, his emphasis was on getting me to a point where normal everyday actions would be within my grasp. So, rather than come in with some hi-tech gadget to hone my fine motor skills, he brought me a nut and a half-inch bolt. It was fiddly to thread the two together with my left hand. Simply holding them between the fingers and thumb on my right proved almost impossible at first. And yet, rolling them over and over during the hours I was alone finally started to pay dividends.

However, working too hard without supervision was, in itself, a potential danger, especially if I wore myself out. To guard against this, my blood sugar levels were checked every six hours by a nurse who took her samples by pricking my fingertip. That was annoying enough during the day, but I got really frustrated when I woke up each night to see the needle coming back out of my skin. Still, I guess that's why it's called 'acute rehab' rather than 'casual convalescence'.

The third member of my rehab team, speech therapist Melanie Romain, was arguably the most important of all. By now, apart from my diapers, the feeding tube in my stomach was the only visible sign that I was still far from well. It was part of Melanie's remit to get that out of me as quickly as possible by fast-tracking my eating programme. In order to do this, I needed stronger throat muscles and greater lung capacity. She had exercises for both, although one was far more controversial than the other. In the meantime, I would continue to be fed mainly through the tube, with top-ups from my mouth as and when I could manage it.

To increase the power of my breaths, Melanie brought in some little balls of cotton wool on a tray. She put the tray on my lap, handed me a straw, and said, 'Blow the balls off the tray.'

It sounded easy. It looked easy. But could I do it? Not easily at all. Not at first, at least. That's how little puff I had after so many months not using my own windpipe.

Failing at blow football might have been disappointing, but Melanie's technique for working my throat muscles was positively scary. By wrapping a special collar round my throat, she was able to pulse electrical stimulation into me, theoretically triggering the muscles into a more dynamic contraction-and-expansion workout than just speaking or breathing could achieve. I can't say it was a pleasant experience, especially when the voltage was turned up to the maximum I could stand, but it didn't hurt. And I had so much faith in Melanie that I wouldn't have complained even if it had.

The scientific approach was clearly her thing. Before she began trying to improve my eating I was taken to the X-ray department and fed a little piece of mushy banana containing some barium dye. As the food passed down my oesophagus, the barium showed up on the monitor so Melanie and her colleagues could see exactly how it was progressing. I was lucky she took that precaution. The dye was clearly heading down my windpipe, as well as my oesophagus, because my throat muscles hadn't sealed it off completely. If I'd tried to eat anything more solid, I would have been in serious trouble. Only once she was satisfied I wasn't swallowing into my windpipe did Melanie move me on to more substantial food. I progressed from the familiar yoghurt and banana to tuna and some small vegetables and egg salad.

I really couldn't have done any more in my first week, so by the end of it I was not surprised to hear that I'd met the insurance company's 25 per cent improvement criterion and could stay. Thereafter, I continued to improve at such a rate that I received some unexpected news at the end of the second week.

'You're progressing so well that we're going to keep you in for one more week,' my doctor revealed. 'Let's do everything we can over the next seven days to get you home.'

'Amen to that,' I replied. 'Just show me what to do.'

Everything stepped up during that bonus week. After another successful dye test, Melanie asked me, 'What would you most like to eat?'

I didn't even have to think about it.

'I'd kill for a cheeseburger right now.'

'Okay,' she said. 'Coming right up.'

I didn't actually see her again until the following morning, but, true to her word, she was carrying a McDonald's bag.

'One cheeseburger. With fries.'

I was so amazed at the sight of my favourite guilty-pleasure fast food that I didn't even worry about whether I could get it down. Half an hour later, the bag was empty and Melanie was smiling. The next day, as another treat, she brought me a slice of homemade chocolate peanut butter pie. When that went down as well, she declared that I was obviously ready for the next stage of my rehab.

'Now it's your turn to cook.'

I was now into the advanced stage of my rehab schedule. Melanie told me that in order to prove I was ready for real, practical life in the outside world I would have to produce a meal for the staff – from scratch. I was given some money, driven to a grocery store by Paul, and had my wheelchair hooked up to a disability trolley. Then, with Paul standing nearby but not helping, I pushed myself around the store, collecting everything I would need to make some meatloaf patties. Back in the kitchen suite of the rehab centre, I chopped the onion and red bell peppers, seasoned the meat and got cooking, sitting in my wheelchair the whole time. An hour later, half a dozen satisfied faces congratulated me on my dish.

With the wheelchair still such an important part of my life, and with my final week in full swing, Mike started doing some serious work on my legs. His approach was slightly less scientific than Melanie's, but he achieved similarly impressive results. While I stood in my walker, Mike would hand me one end of a rope and hold the other end as he sat down in an office chair. Then, on the command of 'Go!', I had to start pulling man and chair towards the door. We didn't move for ages, and I even checked that his chair did indeed have wheels. But then it started inching forwards and we were off. It was incredibly motivational having him sitting right beside me while I walked. Obviously I would never have to drag anyone around on an office chair at home, but I could appreciate why Mike had encouraged me to do it. The sense of achievement was enormous. I felt like the world's strongest man pulling a 747.

For Paul, meanwhile, the specific challenges of my own home became the priority. There was only one way he could learn what those challenges were, and that was by taking a look himself. So it was that one afternoon he drove up to Alta Heights.

And he took me with him!

I got a bit choked as we slowed down on East Avenue. As Paul swung into the drive I remembered the last time I'd done that, on my Harley, on that sunny Tuesday afternoon back in May. It seemed like a lifetime ago, and I sighed with the realisation that

my motorcycling days were long behind me now. But one glimpse of the house and my spirits shot right back up.

'I never thought I'd see this place again,' I said, as Paul lifted me out of the car.

'Well, you'll be seeing it every day pretty soon,' he laughed.

He was there to check exactly how many steps I needed to climb in order to enter the house (five) and to identify any other potential obstacles, such as the fact that we only have a shower in the bath, not a separate stall. But all I could think was, *I'm home. I'm really home.*

It was an emotional moment. Sensing that, Paul asked if I'd like to stay a while once he'd finished. 'If Lili can drive you back later, it's all right with me.'

I could have hugged him. The chance to sit in my lounge on my chair surrounded by my books with my wife meant more than he could ever know. I loved every moment of it.

I'm so lucky to be here.

I knew I was also lucky to have people like Paul on my side. Back at the unit I was put through an intensive programme of stair climbing. As we had five steps at home, Mike wouldn't let me rest until I could comfortably get up six without a break. Similarly, they managed to recreate the exact height and layout of my bath so I was able to practise getting in and out and using the handheld shower from a seated position. The attention to detail was incredible. By the end of the week, I couldn't think of a single extra thing they could possibly have done for me.

Of course, working with mock-up scenarios was one thing. Getting into a real bath with real water at home was going to be a very different story. Just as climbing those steps was going to seem like scaling Everest. Was I really ready to do it? Was I ready to face the real world again?

There was only one way to find out.

CHAPTER TWENTY-ONE

This Can't Be for Me

The grass looks like it could do with some water. The rose bushes need pruning back, ready for winter. There are more oak leaves on the driveway than on the tree. So many things to do. But I couldn't be happier.

The oak could have fallen down and I'd still be happy to see it. I'm happy to see anything that reminds me I'm home.

For good.

I t was the day I hadn't dared to dream would ever happen. Yet it was here. I was home. I was with Lili, ready to embark on the next stage of our life together.

So why was I so scared?

It wasn't easy coming out of the cocoon of the healthcare system. It was 9 October 2009. For almost five months I'd been surrounded by the best medical resources (insurance) money could buy. I'd had people to help me breathe, help me pee, help me swallow. Teams of experienced professionals had monitored me, exercised me and encouraged me. Now I had only one – and that was only because I was married to her.

Actually, Lili did have one ally as far as my ongoing treatment was concerned. Melanie Romain's speech therapy had been so wonderful in the acute rehab unit that my first action after leaving the Queen of the Valley was to enlist her on a private contract to help me progress at home.

On a day-to-day basis, it was another Melanie, my youngest daughter, who took it in turns with a professional carer called Reina to come in and look after me from seven in the morning till seven at night. Lili came home at about five-thirty, which gave her a little private time before she had to take over the caring responsibilities. It was a very comfortable set-up, at least for me.

I owe my Melanie so much. In order to care for me, she moved her entire family out to California. I never asked her to do that. In fact, I never even contributed to the debate. Once she decided, that was it.

While I couldn't have been more comfortable, Lili suddenly had more on her plate than ever. With the feeding tube still connected to my stomach, I couldn't sleep in our normal bed, so she ordered a hospital bed, complete with high sides and wheels, and installed it in the lounge. I'm sure she was grateful that the long commute to Care Meridian was a thing of the past, but the way all our furniture was now stacked higgledy-piggledy left me feeling guilty.

Not that Lili ever mentioned it, of course. In fact, I never once saw her without a smile on her face. I knew how she felt. Five months earlier we'd both faced the prospect that my life and our lives together were over. Every day that had passed since then had brought some improvement, be it tiny or huge. We were grateful for that. Whatever tribulations we had to face now were nothing compared with the road we'd already travelled.

And yet, within four weeks of first crashing around the house with a walker, I was starting to lose my patience. What was the point of being able to go to the bathroom unaided if I still couldn't shut the door because the walker was in the way? It was one week-end, with Lili home during the day, when I said, 'I'm done with this thing. It's going in the shed.'

'Are you sure, honey?' she asked.

'Never been surer of anything. I just need it for one more thing.'

That afternoon, Lili drove me to a store and I invested in a good, solid walking cane. When we got home, she lugged the walker to the shed, as requested – and I haven't laid eyes on it since.

Being able to use a cane was as big a leap forward as using the walker for the first time. Of course, it was much harder, especially as I could now support myself with only one arm, so I needed to work on my balance. But there was no shortage of surfaces in the house to lean on, if necessary. And if there was one thing I'd learned over the last few months, it was that I needed a goal to aim for.

The walker wasn't the only thing I said goodbye to that week. On my weekly outpatients visit to the doctor he asked how my eating was doing.

'Thanks to Melanie Romain's work with me, it's pretty good, actually.'

'So you'll be ready for Thanksgiving, then?'

I laughed. Not so long ago, I'd thought I'd seen my last Thanksgiving. Even if I managed only a sliver of turkey this year, I would enjoy myself like never before.

'Well,' the doctor added, 'you'll probably enjoy yourself even more without the feeding tube. How do you feel about it coming out?'

How do I feel about it? Pulling it out will hurt like hell, I'm sure of that.

I waited for the doctor to say when he could book me in for

the surgery. Instead, he simply reached under my shirt and gave a tug. A few seconds later he was holding the entire coiled tube and a nurse was sticking a large plaster over the exposed aperture in my skin. It hadn't hurt a bit. In fact, far from pain, seeing it in the doctor's hands gave me a massive shot of adrenaline.

That's it. That's the final piece of the puzzle.

Back home, I couldn't wait for nighttime. The feeding hose had been the only thing keeping me from the marital bed. With it gone, Lili and I could at least start moving towards a normal life again. Unfortunately, the moment I tried to lie down, I realised there was going to be another hitch.

'It hurts, Lili,' I said. 'My back hurts when I lie down.'

I'd been propped in a bed at thirty-five degrees for so long that the simple act of lying completely flat was agony. I persevered but in the end I had to accept that the only thing I could do was continue to sleep in the hospital bed and gradually lower its incline in increments over the course of the next few weeks.

It was an annoying setback, but trivial compared with everything else I'd been through. Also, I had more pressing problems to worry about.

The cane that I'd bought was paid for out of my own money. My healthworkers, Melanie and Reina, were both on private contracts paid for by me (thank goodness my daughter Melanie's time was free). On top of that, the insurance company had paid for only 80 per cent of the treatment I'd received at Care Meridian, so I now faced a hefty bill for the remaining fifth. It could have been much worse – for instance, my initial treatment at The Queen's ICU had cost $250,000, which my insurance had covered in full – but I was still in no position to pay and have something left to live on. When all of my bills were settled I had a debt of $15,000 and no income to service it.

It was my daughters who came up with a solution. Melanie and Shannon were visiting one day when they said they were planning to organise a spaghetti drive – a charity event centred on a meal – to raise some money towards my bills. If they charged $10 a head, they thought they could raise about $1,000. I was so proud of them, especially when they said it would be just the first of many events to bring in as much as possible.

'Anything that you girls can do to help would be great,' I said.

To maximise the proceeds of the first event, they approached all of our mutual friends and asked them to sound out potential interest. I don't think anyone anticipated how successful their efforts would be. One person who heard about it, a businessman called Gary Thompson, was so taken by the idea that he got in touch to ask if he could do more than just attend. With my daughters' blessing, he turned his impressive entrepreneurial talents to my plight and organised something a little bigger than a spaghetti drive.

On 2 November, not even a month after my discharge from the Queen of the Valley, I was sitting at home, fully dressed, waiting for the sound of Lili's Mustang in the drive. It was a Monday night and I knew a party had already started in the large function room at the Artesa Winery. Actually, it was more than a party. It was a benefit. But this wasn't a fundraiser for a presidential candidate. It was for me.

I had no idea how Gary had done it, but he'd managed to get the premises for free for the night, he'd persuaded some incredible restaurants to donate the catering, and he'd recruited dozens of volunteers to ensure the whole evening ran smoothly. He'd also pulled in dozens of amazing prizes, from a holiday for six in Hawaii to exclusive restaurant seats, for a silent auction, had laid on a band, and, on top of all that, was charging $50 a ticket – with every single penny raised destined for my medical fund.

Sadly, I didn't have the strength to attend from start to finish, but knowing that so many friends, family and, I was told, strangers were working so hard on my behalf, I at least had to make an appearance. On the way to the winery, Lili filled me in on the sheer scale of the event. I was incredulous, but she swore she wasn't exaggerating.

When we finally arrived, the second I stepped inside that room I was blown away. There were hundreds of people there, eating, laughing, dancing and having a whale of a time. For a moment I froze on my cane.

I must have the wrong room. This can't be for me.

I looked at Lili and she shrugged as if to say, 'Told you,' but I'm sure it was just as bizarre for her. At that moment, I think we both would have been more comfortable just slipping out again.

But that wasn't to be.

'Hey, look, it's Rich!'

Keith Reuter's unmistakable voice boomed out across the hall. I'd been spotted. There was no hiding now.

I could tell that Keith's instincts were to rush over, but a sharp look from Lili made everyone stand back. Luckily, with the band belting out a tune, only the tables by the door were aware that I'd arrived, but even the stares and hellos from thirty or forty people felt just the wrong side of intimidating.

I managed to stay for about half an hour, seated and surrounded. Months of having people visit me in hospital had not prepared me for this, and, despite seeing the faces of the people I loved most in the world, I couldn't wait to escape. Before I did, however, I noticed the band had come to a halt. Someone must

have passed a note to the singer because he was informing the
room of the arrival of a very special guest.

Oh hell …

I felt such a heel leaving, but if you have to go, going with an
almighty roar of goodwill from a room full of wonderful people is
certainly the way to do it. My head was buzzing with shock for the
rest of the evening. And the next morning I couldn't help wondering if it had all been a dream.

I was so stunned by the outpouring of support in that room
that I completely forgot why the event had been held in the first
place. So when Gary Thompson called round a week or so later, I
thought he was just giving me the opportunity to thank him in
person. When he pulled out a cheque payable to me I nearly
fainted.

The number on it was $20,000.

No words could express how I felt at that moment. I barely
knew this man, we were friends of friends at best, yet he'd done so
much for me.

'How can I ever repay you, Gary?'

'Just continue to get better, Rich. That's all anyone wants
from you.'

'I'll do that, Gary. I promise I will.'

You Can Consider Yourself
Very Lucky

I kept my promise to Gary. Or, at least, I tried.

As I sat down with Lili for a quiet Christmas Day dinner seven weeks after the fundraiser, I reflected on how my cane had already joined the walker out in the shed. I reflected on how our lounge was back to normal now that I was sleeping as happily as ever in my own bed. And I reflected on how the doctors at the Queen of the Valley had said they'd never seen anyone achieve my level and speed of recovery. I was, they estimated, already at 95 per cent of where I'd been before the stroke.

But that was not the end of the story.

I was still clawing back more of my independence day by day the following year, but then, on 4 July 2010, I felt a familiar sensation. In fact, I felt it twice. A visit to the hospital confirmed what I'd been dreading. I'd had two 'mini-strokes'. That wouldn't be good news for anyone. For someone with my history, it seemed like the final throw of the dice.

A neurologist sat me down in his office and told me, 'I've reviewed your latest CAT scan and it appears your basilar artery is totally blocked. There is no blood going to the back of your brain.'

He might as well have said, 'You're going to die soon.'

That was what everyone in the room – me, Lili, Melanie and Shannon – heard anyway. After everything we'd gone through to fight the original clot, this was just too much. Tears were shed, words escaped us. All hope flew out of the window.

Told my chances of survival were, once again, zero, we were advised to consult a neurosurgeon. She was only marginally more optimistic: 'Your basilar artery is either blocked or collapsed. We're going to perform an angiogram to establish which, because if it's collapsed, we can repair it. If it is blocked, however, I'm afraid the outlook isn't so good.'

In other words, I'm doomed.

Waiting for the result of the angiogram was like waiting to be given a time for my execution. It wasn't a case of *will* I die but *when*?

Finally, the neurosurgeon returned. 'I have some good news and some bad news,' she said. 'The bad news is that your basilar artery is completely blocked.'

Feeling the need to prove it, she held up the X-rays for us to examine. I didn't know exactly what I was looking at, but I knew it was killing me. I completely forgot that she'd promised good news, too.

'However,' the doctor continued, pointing to a dark line on the plastic sheet, 'your carotid arteries on both sides have branched off.'

'What does that mean?' Lili asked, on behalf of us all.

'It means that they are now bypassing the clot and supplying blood to the back of your brain. I can't explain how that has happened, but this is the reason why you are still alive.'

I couldn't believe it. Another miracle. A year ago I'd come back from the dead and now I'd survived two more supposedly fatal attacks. Either one of the mini-strokes should have killed me.

'You can consider yourself very lucky, Richard.'

'Oh, I do, Doctor, you can be assured of that.'

And not just because of my health. Yes, I was a walking resurrection. Yes, I had defied the odds once and then did it again. But I was only happy because I had something wonderful to live for. My near-death experience had brought my entire family together. Lili, Shannon, Melanie and Michelle – the four most important people in my life – were all tied tight together now as a unit. Melanie had even moved her entire family just to be near me. I couldn't ask for more from any of them.

As I write, three years later, nothing has changed. Officially, I'm still operating at only 95 per cent capacity, but – you know what? – I am happy with that. I'm back in the gym every day, I cycle everywhere and I'm generally as active as I've ever been. Occasionally I stumble over a word or two, my balance isn't as solid as it once was and I'm much more trigger-happy where tears are concerned. Other than that, though, you would never guess that I'd had three strokes and had watched a doctor advise my wife to turn off my life-support machines.

Not everyone is as lucky as I am. In fact, hardly anyone is. The list of those who have emerged from locked-in syndrome is microscopically small, and the life expectancy of those who remain trapped is still desperately short. Nevertheless, awareness of the condition is slowly increasing because of the determination of several sufferers.

In the UK in 2012, a supremely brave man called Tony Nicklinson lost his long legal battle for an assisted death seven years after he had become trapped in his body as a result of locked-in syndrome. In a final act of independence, he went on hunger strike and in August of that year finally found the peace he craved. Impressively, his family continue to campaign in Tony's name so that locked-in sufferers may eventually have the freedom to choose when they die. If I had been in Tony's position, faced with a life-time on machinery, I think I would have taken the same route.

I never met Tony, but I've made it my duty to contact other sufferers and show them there is another way. I have a friend in San Francisco who has been locked in since September 2011. She has not made much improvement since then, and it's hard for her family to believe she's really still in there. But I'm living proof that they should never give up on her. They already use a spell board, and they're trying to raise the money to buy an electronic talking aid, too. As so often in the US healthcare system, though, a lack of money is holding them back.

There's a shortage of information, too. When I was at The Queen, and later in the Facility and Care Meridian, my family scoured the book stores for some – *any* – information on what they might expect over the coming months. They returned empty-handed every time. Numerous searches on the internet proved equally frustrating. That was one reason why I wrote this book. It is my guide to what it feels like on the inside looking out – and what it's like for the loved ones looking in.

Another reason was to help spread awareness of the problem. How many locked-in patients have been misdiagnosed as brain-dead coma victims, dismissed as 'vegetables', and had their life support shut down? Doctors and families need to be aware that another check should always be made before the plug is pulled. And then another, and another, and another . . .

Ultimately, I owe my second life to the faith so many people showed in me. My wife and family, of course, my medics and the wonderful therapists at The Queen, the Facility and Care Meridian, but also Gary Thompson and each and every one of the well-wishers who gathered to raise funds for my rehabilitation. Without their unflinching support, I don't think I could have carried on.

Because, after all, life is worth living only if you enjoy it and you're not a burden on the ones you love. Fortunately, I got back to loving life some time ago, and I continue to do so now thanks to the wonderful people around me.

As an example of just how lucky I am, a few days after the benefit held in my honour, Keith and Pam Reuter came to visit. After we'd chatted about how my recovery was progressing and what a great night the fundraiser had been, they casually told me that they'd bid for several items in the silent auction. It turned out they'd won the big one – the trip for six to Hawaii – and had already invited another couple.

'But that means there are still two places up for grabs,' Keith explained. 'How do you and Lili fancy it, Rich? Do you think you'll be well enough to come with us?'

A trip to Hawaii? With my closest friends? If I needed any more motivation to get better, that was it. In September 2010, we all boarded the plane.

I haven't looked back since.